RUNAWAY GIRL

The Artist Louise Bourgeois

JAN GREENBERG AND SANDRA JORDAN

Harry N. Abrams, Inc., Publishers

LIBRARY
FRANKLIN PIERCE COLLEGE
RINDGE, NH 03461

COVER: *(UPPER)* **Louise Bourgeois in the studio of her apartment at East 18th Street, NYC, circa 1946;** *(LOWER)* **Louise in Paris, circa 1932**
BACK COVER: **Louise with Spider IV in 1996,** Photo: Peter Bellamy
TITLE PAGE: **Louise in 1992 with a portrait of her by photographer Berenice Abbott circa 1949 in the background.** *Photograph © Yosef Adar, courtesy of Louise Bourgeois.*

Designer: Anna Christian
Production Director: Hope Koturo

Library of Congress Cataloging-in-Publication Data

Greenberg, Jan, 1942–
    Runaway girl : the artist Louise Bourgeois / by Jan Greenberg and Sandra Jordan.
        p. cm.
    Summary: Introduces the life of renowned modern artist Louise Bourgeois,
    who is known primarily for her sculptures.
    Includes bibliographical references and index.
    ISBN 0-8109-4237-2
    1. Bourgeois, Louise, 1911—Juvenile literature. 2. Artists—United States—
    Biography—Juvenile literature. [1. Bourgeois, Louise, 1911–
    2. Artists. 3. Women—Biography.] I. Jordan, Sandra (Sandra Jane Fairfax)
    II. Title.
    N6537.B645 G74 2003
    730'.92—dc21

                                            2002011922

Text copyright © 2003 Jan Greenberg and Sandra Jordan
Excerpts and works of art by Louise Bourgeois © 2003 Louise Bourgeois
All other copyright notices appear alongside the reproduction or on page 75.

Published in 2003 by Harry N. Abrams, Incorporated, New York
All rights reserved. No part of the contents of this book may be
reproduced without the written permission of the publisher.

Printed and bound in China
10 9 8 7 6 5 4 3 2 1

Harry N. Abrams, Inc.
100 Fifth Avenue
New York, N.Y. 10011
www.abramsbooks.com

Abrams is a subsidiary of

To my new muse, Colette. *Bienvenue.*

—J. G.

For my amazing writers' group. Friends till the end.
Bonnie Bryant, Miriam Cohen, Peter Lerangis, Ellen Levine, Fran Manushkin,
Norma Fox Mazer, Harry Mazer, Barbara Seuling, Marvin Terban

—S. J.

Champfleurette #2, 1999

Contents

ONE *Family Tapestry* 7

TWO *Family Secrets* 15

THREE *A Young Artist in Paris* 27

FOUR *Runaway Girl* 33

FIVE *The New York Art Scene* 45

SIX *The Great Decade* 53

SEVEN *Spider, Spider, Burning Bright* 61

Important Dates 66

How to Look at a Sculpture 68

Where to View Artwork by Louise Bourgeois 69

Glossary 70

Bibliography 72

Endnotes 72

List of Artworks in Chronological Order 74

List of Artworks by Chapter 75

Photography Credits 77

Acknowledgments 78

Index 80

Louise working on a plaster sculpture in Italy, 1967

*"I was in effect
a runaway girl.
I was a runaway
girl who turned
out all right."*
—Louise Bourgeois

CHAPTER ONE

FAMILY TAPESTRY

In an old town house on a tree-lined street in New York City, we sit waiting to meet Louise Bourgeois, one of the world's leading artists. She has said, "In my art I am the murderer. As an artist I am a powerful person. In real life, I feel like the mouse behind the radiator." We are here to find out what she means. There is a slight rustling from the kitchen. Is she listening to us, deciding if she will come out? Louise has a reputation for saying exactly what's on her mind. And she's been known to ask interviewers to leave if she doesn't like their questions. Suddenly she appears, fragile and petite, dressed in layers of quilted cotton. With her soft French accent and wry smile, Louise at ninety still retains a girlish presence. Her pale blue eyes miss

Louise's home on West 20th Street, NYC

nothing, and her responses to questions are sharp and tinged with humor. She asks her longtime assistant, Jerry Gorovoy, to bring out a pile of scrapbooks made of heavy, dark, embossed leather. She opens one. "My father was an amateur photographer, always taking pictures," she explains. We peer closely at the small sepia images. There is young Louise, standing proudly on a chair, dressed in a velvet coat and laced-up boots. Her parents, her brother and sister, friends, houses, trips fill the album's pages. She says, "All my work in the past fifty years, all my subjects, have found their inspiration in my childhood. My childhood never lost its magic, it has never lost its mystery, and it has never lost its drama."

ouise Bourgeois was born in 1911, on Christmas Day in Paris. She claims her arrival was not an entirely joyous event. "I was a pain in the ass when I was born. All these people had their oysters and champagne, and there I came. My mother was very apologetic and the doctor said, 'Madame Bourgeois, really, you are ruining my festivity.'" Not only did Louise interrupt the Christmas party, but even worse, she was the wrong sex. The Bourgeois family already had a daughter. "When I was born my father and mother were fighting like cats and dogs. And the country was preparing for war, and my father, who wanted a son, got me." For Louise this inconvenient birth was the beginning of a turbulent story that would shape her art.

Within three years, in 1914, World War I broke out and German tanks rolled into France. Louise's father enlisted in the French army and immediately was sent to fight. To keep Louise, her older sister, Henriette, and baby brother, Pierre, out of danger, their mother, Joséphine, moved them from Choisy-le-Roi, their handsome residence outside

Louise in profile on her mother's lap in front of the family house in Choisy-le-Roi, about 1914

Louise restoring a tapestry fragment in 1990

of Paris, to Aubusson, the town where her family lived "in a large and forbidding house." Joséphine Bourgeois had spent her childhood there, learning the tapestry trade that had been the family business for generations. She hoped in Aubusson the children would be safe. In spite of the move, many of Louise's earliest and most vivid memories were of war. A railroad line ran near the house. As she lay in her bed at night, she heard through her bedroom window the cries of wounded soldiers passing by in trains from the battle front. The sounds mingled with the odor from the town's slaughterhouse across the street.

At three years old, Louise understood little about politics or war. She only knew her mother spent nights weeping and her father was gone. Louise felt abandoned by him. Joséphine, hysterical with worry, especially if she did not receive a daily letter from her husband, dragged Louise along to visit him at army camps, leaving the other children at home. Louise said, "I was the favorite because I looked most like him." When the news came that Louis was wounded, Joséphine and Louise went immediately to the hospital. Louis recovered and was sent back to fight. But Louise never forgot the sight of hospital beds filled with soldiers—their shattered limbs and bloody bandages.

When the war ended and her father at last returned home, the family bought a spacious house with gardens that ran down to the Bièvre River in the town of Antony. The roots of plants that grew along the riverbanks gave the water a special chemical consistency called tannin, necessary for dying tapestry wool. There the Bourgeoises would continue in the tapestry business, finding and restoring sixteenth- and seventeenth-century textiles and selling them to collectors from their gallery in Paris. These handwoven wall hangings, once necessary to keep stone walls in castles warm, had been out of fashion for hundreds of years. However, thrifty, practical farm families of France did not throw out such richly decorated fabric. Instead,

The family house in Antony, outside of Paris, 1932

they used it wherever heavy, well-made cloth was needed—for curtains or to protect animals during the cold winters. Louis Bourgeois searched farmhouses, crumbling châteaus, and stables for the tattered fragments. The scenes woven into the tapestries most often illustrated stories from the Bible or Greek and Roman myths. Joséphine arranged the remnants on shelves by theme. Sections separated for many years were reunited in their *atelier* (studio).

The tapestry workshop took up part of the house in Antony, where Joséphine supervised a staff of twenty-five women. The rhythms of the business punctuated Louise's daily life. She played by the river where the laundry workers knelt in wood boxes to shield them from the current, washing tapestries that grew heavy with river water. She saw the carefully tended pots of dye bubbling on the gas stove in the kitchen and the skeins of dyed wool hanging in the garden to dry. She watched the seamstresses spread the torn fabric face-down on a huge table, thread their needles with yarn, and begin stitching and reweaving it back to its original glory. "I've always had a fascination with the needle," she said. "The magic power of the needle. The needle is used to repair the damage."

On his travels Louis Bourgeois collected not only tapestries but also eighteenth-century garden statues made of thin lead. Their crumpled limbs, in constant need of repair, littered the garden. His other passion was fine old furniture. Louise liked to go up to

Tapestry workers in the washhouse on the Bièvre River in 1920

The Garden

"Each of us, my sister, my brother and I had a garden and we tried to make the most of it, learning the art of cutting trees, espaliering pears and apples. They were formal gardens, with roses in certain areas marked off by boxwood. I was hardworking, interested in that garden. And I had a passion for rock collecting. I began with granite and moved on, through studying geology, to other kinds of rock.

"But that garden had another importance for me. We had a tent at the bottom of it, and sometimes we would sleep there. Often we took our meals there, and then we had to carry all the food out from the kitchen and back. Dinner was served late, and night would surprise us as we were eating. Then you could look back and see the light of the kitchen, only far away through the trees.

"And then our father would often say, 'Now, I don't want to have children who are afraid, so you are going to go to the kitchen and bring the salt shaker.' So my brother and I would run, terrified. We would take different ways back, and I would end up at the kitchen door. There was always a man there, the man who took care of the sheep and the pig. He would say, 'You are not supposed to come into the kitchen!' The reason was that he had been kissing the cook. Then both of them would say things to make me blush. It seems to me now that our father did this to test us, knowing, among other things, that we children were afraid of the dark."

Red Room (Child), *(detail) 1994, an installation (with large spools of thread) that draws on memories from Louise's childhood more than seventy years ago*

From an early age Louise kept journals and notebooks filled with her drawing, sketches, and writing.

_____

"Now obviously, this is a self-portrait, and there I am climbing the mountain in my best appearance. It's a very formal and abstract representation of a person. You see, it took me a long time to get there, so the white shape at the top is actually the shape of the hair; the hair is blown, and it is a very flattering portrait. I appear very pleased with myself."
—From *Drawings & Observations*

Untitled, *1944*

Passage Dangereux, *1997, an installation with hanging chairs*

the large attic where, high above the bare wood floors, hung the frames of antique wood armchairs stripped of their fabric. "It was quite impressive. This is the origin of a lot of hanging pieces," she said, referring to her art.

Louise's parents, although they lived a comfortable life, were entrepreneurs, not French aristocrats. Together, they combined their individual talents to keep the tapestry business going. "My parents worked together. They appreciated each other and were indispensable to each other."

Louise worked as hard as her parents, always seeking their approval. "At school, art was important and from the beginning I was an overachiever. That is to say, if you flatter me, or look at me the right way, I will kill myself to please you. It's very painful to be an overachiever. Anyway, in art class I was not better than anybody else, to tell you the truth—but I tried to make believe that I was. And I worked like a dog."

One day a draftsman, whose special job it was to fill in the missing areas of the tapestry, did not show up. Joséphine said to her ten-year-old daughter, "Since you make drawings all the time, why don't you help me make a drawing on this tapestry so we can go on." Louise had been teased by her father that she was "a useless mouth," meaning she needed to be fed but contributed nothing in return. "And I was supposed to make myself forgiven for being a girl." Cautiously she made a sketch. To her relief, everyone thought her feet were wonderful. "It was," Louise said, "a great victory." From that time on, she helped out in the atelier, as well as attended private school in nearby Paris. Since the tapestries were torn at the bottom from dragging on the floor, the feet on the figures often were missing. "I became an expert at drawing legs and feet. I still do it: I still do lots of feet. . . . It taught me that art could be interesting, as well as useful. That is how my art started."

"You see. I have to feel—in order to be a decent person—that my parents are on my side. They do not criticize me; they don't find me ugly. They seem to endorse me, for better or for worse."

—Louise Bourgeois

CHAPTER TWO

FAMILY SECRETS

Photographs of Louise's father show a dapper, handsome man, often surrounded by his well-dressed family on vacations in the south of France, in Paris, and at their large, rambling house. From these pictures it looks as if Louise spent an enchanted childhood presided over by a confident, elegant father. But there was a dark side to Louis Bourgeois.

At home he sat at the head of the dinner table. Around him

Orange Episode, *1990*

assembled the family, Louise, her mother, sister, brother, and two young cousins whose father had been killed in the war. A pile of cheap plates were stacked at his elbow, placed there by Louise's mother so he could smash saucers instead of yelling at the children. Her father dominated the conversation, Louise said, "bragging and talking about how wonderful he is." After dinner everyone at the table was expected to perform by singing a song or reciting a poem.

One night for his entertainment, her father peeled an orange with a knife, cutting from it a small figure he claimed was a portrait of Louise—her head, a pair of wings or huge ears, two breasts, legs and feet. "But wait," he said, as the pith of the orange came out with a long twirl between its legs. "Look at this splendid thing. Louise has nothing down there. It can't be my daughter after all!"

Louise felt humiliated by his teasing, ashamed not to be the boy he always wanted. Sometimes she countered her father's displays by throwing a tantrum. But this time she didn't confront him or make a scene. "I took white bread, mixed it with spit and molded a figure of my father. When the figure was done I started cutting off the limbs with a knife." She called it, *"une poupée de pain"* (a play on the French word for bread: *pain*)."

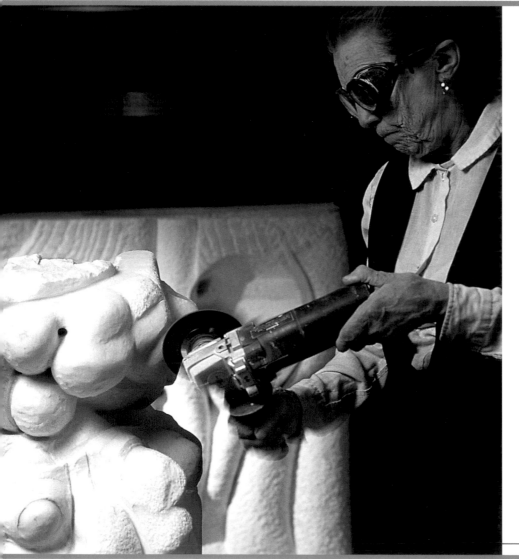

Talking with Louise Bourgeois

For more than forty years Louise has lived in a four-story brick town house in Chelsea, an old section of New York. Paint is peeling off the walls, and the floors are scuffed. Luxurious living doesn't interest this famous artist. She has her work, she says, and that's all she needs. On a table is a metronome and an empty flask of Shalimar perfume, both objects that have been used in recent artworks. A semi-circle of mismatched chairs awaits the arrival of the young artists and poets invited to share their work at her Sunday salons. Louise knows some of her answers are outrageous, and she follows them up with a sidelong glance. But always there is a sense of serious purpose and confidence in what she says.

Louise in her studio in 1988

"A doll of bread. A doll of pain." One day Louise would make sculpture in many materials other than humble bread—from rubber, plaster, and latex to bronze and marble—but the anger that prompted her first artwork would resurface again and again in her life. Just as a songwriter might turn a heartbreak into lyrics or a poet, verse, Louise relieved her anger and transformed it into art. "Art is the promise the artist makes to the community that they will not commit murder," she said.

Fifty years later, in her studio, recalling her helpless rage, she used it to produce a striking artwork. Even though she is a vegetarian, she went to the butcher and bought cuts of beef and lamb shoulders, shoved them into plaster of paris, and made molds.

JAN AND SANDRA: **Where do you get your ideas?**

LOUISE: *My inspiration comes from the beauty of the past. That's where I am completely omnipotent. Our past is ours. Sometimes you have good memories, sometimes you have bad memories, but they are your memories.*

J AND S: **Tell us about *The Destruction of the Father* and how it relates to your relationship with your parents.**

LOUISE: *When you are at a certain age . . . I don't say in a certain mood . . . I would say at a certain age of your development . . . you want to get rid of the parents, never hear about them and enjoy destroying them. But this is not the whole thing. Two or three years later you are a different person, . . . you have your own children or whatever, and you think the parents after all were not that bad. Or maybe they were pretty bad but not all the time. So then you make a piece which is the rebuilding or the improving of the parents. So the* Destruction of the Father *is very important*

to me. It is a subject that goes back to my teens. It goes back to what I felt at the time. I felt very good to have killed them off—and very good to have rebuilt them.

J AND S: **You have talked about fear and working through the fear.**

LOUISE: *The fear comes in when you talk about feelings and about omnipotence, massacre, violence. Then you feel a terrible fear. Well, it's normal that you are afraid, considering what you fantasized. When the world of fantasy and wishes goes beyond the limits of what's reasonable, the fear strikes. Fear leads into depression. So you should be very careful to keep a balance. The work says, "Now Louise, do not go overboard in hating, in loving. Just be a little bit more level." The work is about pulling back and finding a little balance for all these feelings.*

J AND S: **So when you take the fear and make art out of it, does the fear go away?**

LOUISE: *I am completely free with my unconscious, which artists are. We have*

access to the unconscious and are fearless. It takes a kind of fearlessness in your art making to cut your parents up into little pieces and put them down the drain. It is in a world of fantasy. But then you wake up, you are afraid of what you've done. But then comes the reparation and exorcism. All my work is that. I start with these incredible murderous scenes. But I won't leave the studio until I've done something to exorcise the murder I've committed. Then I feel fine.

J AND S: **How do you know a piece is finished?**

LOUISE: *It is never finished. The subject is never exhausted.*

———

The phone rings. Jerry Gorovy answers it. An artist wants to come to Louise's Sunday salon. "Let me talk," Louise says. "Who are you? What kind of work do you do? A painter? What size?" She listens for a minute and finally says, "All right. You could come at three o'clock. Don't come if you have a cold."

She cast the shapes, and when they dried, brushed latex over the casts. Then she built a box, a cavelike structure with repetitive bulging shapes, resembling body parts, on the ceiling, floor, and central table of the installation. Across the table she scattered her horrific-looking casts. The red lights that illuminate the sculpture give a threatening look to the whole scene. Louise named it *The Destruction of the Father*. She said, "This piece is basically a table, the awful, terrifying family dinner table headed by the father who sits and gloats. . . . So in exasperation, we grabbed the man, threw him on the table, and dismembered him. . . ."

The artist says the work is about confronting her fear, "ordinary garden variety fear, the actual physical fear I still feel today." We don't have to know her story to have our own

strong reaction. The red stain and threatening shapes make the artist's violent symbolism plain, though she points out that the release of her aggressive feelings is limited to her work. "I'm afraid of power. It makes me nervous. In real life, I identify with the victim; that is why I went into art."

Louise had other reasons to be angry with her father. When Louise was eleven, he hired a young, blonde Englishwoman named

OPPOSITE: *Louise working on* **Destruction of the Father;** RIGHT *(DETAIL, photo: Peter Moore)* AND BELOW: **Destruction of the Father,** *1974*

Sadie Gordon to take care of the children and teach them to speak English. But it was an open secret that Sadie eventually became Louis Bourgeois's mistress. She lived with the family for ten years. Louise remembers going out for drives in the family's big black sedan. Her father and Sadie sat in the front seat with Louise and her mother in the back. Joséphine told her daughter, "Don't worry. When you're eighteen, you can be the driver." But that didn't stop Louise's jealousy at having to compete for her father's attention with an intruder, a girl only seven years older than herself. The household simmered with uneasy feelings.

Even eighty years later, speaking about Sadie, Louise makes a wringing motion with her hands. "As a child, after washing the tapestries in the river, I would twist them with three others or more to wring the water out. Later I would dream of getting rid of my father's mistress. I would do it in my dreams by twisting her neck." She has translated this violent physical act again and again into spiral forms and twisted shapes.

Louise's father told her, "You have to be thankful for me. I brought you into the world. I give you milk and croissants. . . ." Her mother, Joséphine, gave her more practical advice: "Louise, you do not have to fear not to succeed in life, not to find a place for yourself. All you have to do is make yourself indispensable."

**Spiral Woman,
(detail), 1984**

Louise, brother Pierre, and Sadie in a rowboat on the Bièvre River, 1922

Louise's mother, Joséphine, in the family's richly decorated Parisian tapestry gallery, 1911

Louise with Spider IV, *1996. "My best friend was my mother. She was deliberate, clever, patient, soothing, reasonable and dainty, subtle, indispensable, neat and useful as a spider."*

Capable, hardworking, and artistic, Joséphine set a good example. The special dyes she brewed from old herbal recipes helped give the tapestries historical accuracy. Soft rose, moss green, dusky blue—these colors later found their way into Louise's prints and drawings. Joséphine also could be a tough employer. "When my mother said something, the building shook, and my father fled. Even today I am still afraid of

Le Défi, *1991. Small glasses used for cupping are displayed on the bottom glass shelf of a cabinet filled with fragile objects and balanced carefully on one central wheel (not visible).*

what I think of as 'The Angry Mother,'" said Louise. "She had a lot of women working for her, and she had to be forceful." Louise sat for hours in the sewing room, listening to the stories the women spun to amuse themselves as they bent over their weaving. It was through their gossip that Louise learned about her father and Sadie.

Yet Joséphine seems to have accepted Sadie as she accepted most of her husband's extravagant behavior. "How is it that in a middle-class family this mistress is a standard piece of furniture?" asked Louise. "Well, the reason is because my mother tolerated it." Joséphine excused it to her daughter, claiming that men were children who had to be humored. Her attitude may have been influenced by her own delicate health. At the end of World War I, a deadly epidemic called Spanish flu swept around the world. Within three months, more people died of the flu than had been killed in the war. Struck down by it, Joséphine survived, but it left her with a chronic lung problem. To protect her health, the family spent winter months in a warmer climate on the Riviera. It was Louise who traveled with Joséphine and took on the burden of nursing her. "To please my father, I took care of my mother. We treated the tapestries and repaired them. And by extension I treated my mother and tried to repair her. I spent all my time repairing things."

In an old-fashioned medical procedure, Louise heated cups made of strong glass to exhaust the oxygen in the cup and create a vacuum, and then placed them on her mother's

Louise with **The She-Fox**, *1985*

back. In theory, "cupping" expelled the toxins. All it really did was cause red welts on the flesh. Years later, in her sculpture, the glass cups and bottles arranged on shelves and in cell-like structures are an eerie reminder of what must have been a difficult act for the young Louise (see page 23).

What Louise couldn't voice was a deep sense of betrayal—by her mother, who accepted the unacceptable; by Sadie, who was supposed to be her teacher; and by her father, who committed this disloyal and outrageous act. Louise spent her childhood protecting her mother and guarding family secrets. This conflict between love and anger, loyalty and betrayal, the interplay of opposites, found expression in *The She-Fox*, 1985, one of her most famous sculptures. Louise has said, "It is not an image I am seeking. It is not an idea. It is an emotion you want to recreate, an emotion of wanting, of giving, and of destroying." Here the subject is a six-foot-tall animal-like figure carved in black marble. The head is missing, the neck gashed, the body battered and scarred by the artist. "*The She-Fox* is simply my mother," said Louise. "I was preoccupied with the idea that my mother could not possibly love me, and this I could not take." Thus the artist vented her frustration on the artwork. Yet she points out that, in spite of the gouged surface, the piece also is carefully polished. She calls the polishing a "nurturing" act. It is her way of resolving anger and repairing the damage. Sheltered under one paw nestles a smiling figure. "Despite what I was, my mother did love me," said Louise. "As you move up close, you see the little creature is pleased, because she is protected. The murderous creature has no motive except to be loved. The kid is myself."

*"I was looking
for truth,
for people who
weren't phony,
looking for
authenticity."*
—Louise Bourgeois

CHAPTER THREE

A YOUNG ARTIST IN PARIS

Springtime in Paris, 1929. Louise, age eighteen, sat by herself on a park bench watching nannies in their lace caps, laughing children, and white chestnut blossoms. On her lap lay a mathematics text for a class she was taking at the Sorbonne, part of the University of Paris. Here she was, the gifted child of parents who, vying for her affections, each dressed her in clothes from the best French designers. When asked if she was the favored child, she once said,

Cell I, (detail) 1991

"My parents treated me with more respect than my brother and sister because of my abilities and potential." She had tried to satisfy them both, studying diligently for her mother, accompanying her father to the smoke-filled cabarets he liked to frequent at night. Her parents, always demanding, monitored her every move. She had chosen to study mathematics because, unlike the drama of her family life, it followed a reliable system of rules. "It was a world of order that I wanted. I had been in a state of anxiety and needed reassurance."

A portrait of Louise taken by the celebrated French photographer Brassai at the Académie de la Grande-Chaumière, Paris, 1934

Yet Paris offered other diversions for a student beyond the walls of a classroom. It was the place to be in the 1920s for anyone seeking a bohemian life, especially artists and writers. They had invented a movement in art, poetry, and theater, called Surrealism, based on dreams, nightmares, and fantasies—the dark side of human nature. Another group of artists called Dadaists said if a rule existed, it was to be broken. Unrestrained imagination was the only thing that mattered. One of the leaders of Dadaism, Marcel Duchamp, had hung a urinal from the wall, signed it with the name *R. Mutt,* and proclaimed it art. Louise's father called artists "parasites" and discouraged Louise's growing curiosity about modern art.

It would be several years before Louise took her first steps toward independence from her family. Not until her mother died in 1932 did she enroll at the École des Beaux-Arts (School of Fine Arts) and the Académie de la Grande-Chaumière to study art history and art. "Mathematics . . . it simply went into a theoretical world I had no use for." She needed to find a new formula for her life's work, a new equation. "The new equation," she said, "was art."

Her father refused to pay her tuition. To an old-fashioned man who collected antiques and tapestries, modern art was like the Abominable Snowman, to be dismissed as a hoax. His daughter should marry and go into the family business, not waste time

Segmented Wood Personages, *1951,* are reminders of her first discovery of working in three dimensions.

J'y Suis, J'y Reste, **1990. Body parts—hands, feet, and limbs— often appear in Louise's sculpture.**

and money chasing after silly ambitions. Again Louise felt all alone, abandoned by her father, and missing her mother. "I still choke with loneliness remembering those days." But she also remembered her mother's words, "Make yourself indispensable, Louise." A number of good French artists taught art classes to Americans to make extra money. Louise couldn't afford lessons but found a way to be indispensable. She could speak English. So as a translator, she was allowed to join the classes.

Louise made clay figures copied from casts of ancient statues and took a sketch class where "you had to produce something in five minutes." It was an exercise she found liberating after the structured, repetitive exercises taught at the École des Beaux-Arts. In the atelier of the famous painter Fernand Léger, she had a revelation. "It happened this way: one day he took a wood shaving—it was like a lock of hair—and he pinned it up under a shelf where it fell freely in space. We were told to make a drawing of it. I was very interested in the spiral of the shaving, the form it took and its trembling quality." Léger took one look at her drawings and said, "You are not a painter. You are a sculptor."

Later artworks hark back to those wood shavings (see page 29). "Léger made me realize I did not have to be stuck in tapestries and my family, that there was a whole new world in Paris."

Louise took a job as a docent, leading tours at the Musée du Louvre (Louvre museum). Every day she was given an hour lunch break and sent down to the basement of the museum to eat with the staff. Louise said, "If you are wounded in the war in France, you are entitled to an official position. And I walk in and look and a leg is cut off or an arm is gone and they are all in that basement eating their lunch." Again she had come face-to-face with the images of the wounded at the army hospital that had frightened her as a child, another theme that would surface in her artwork. But for now it was impossible to continue working there.

For the next six years her confidence grew as she taught in the art department at the École des Beaux-Arts and toured Europe with fellow students. Of her trips to Russia in the 1930s, she said, "I was attracted to Communism because it bothered my father. I was brought up on teasing and returned the compliment whenever I could." Although she never joined the Communist Party, her two trips to Moscow were another way of rebelling, of proving her independence. She also moved out of her father's house and into her own modest apartment in Paris.

Soon she opened a small art gallery to show contemporary prints and drawings on one side of her father's tapestry shop. Although Louis Bourgeois looked down on artists, he didn't mind the commercial side of art. One day a young American art historian named Robert Goldwater wandered into the gallery and bought two Picasso prints from her. In a letter to a friend Louise wrote, "In between conversations about Surrealism and the latest trends, we got married."

Louise admitted one of her attractions to Robert was that her father didn't approve of him and that "he

Louise and her husband, Robert, in Huntington (Long Island, N.Y.) in 1940

could put my father in his place." She said, "I had met someone who was kind. I felt all was well and I was safe with Robert. And that left me free to begin." In October 1938 she sailed aboard a ship for the United States to reinvent her life in New York.

OPPOSITE AND BELOW:
Louise in her studio, 1946

"Do you know the New York sky? It is outstanding. It is a serious thing. The New York sky is blue, utterly blue. The light is white and the air is strong, and it is healthy too. There is no foolishness about the sky."

—*Louise Bourgeois*

CHAPTER FOUR

RUNAWAY GIRL

What was it about New York City that both energized and disturbed Louise? For one thing it was so different from the wide boulevards, graceful limestone palaces, and cozy parks of Paris. There the Seine River, crisscrossed with cast-iron bridges, wound through the center of the old city. By contrast, New York was raw hustle and bustle, thrusting skyscrapers, crowded asphalt streets, sirens wailing, horns honking, and people rushing everywhere. It was in this complex, energetic, and sometimes violent city that Louise was inspired to make art about "subjects I would have been embarrassed to attempt in Paris." She had run away from the burden of her family history, left it behind in Europe, "to be free, to be as wild as I wanted."

Although Louise and Robert bought a small farmhouse in Connecticut for summers and weekends, she could work only in the city. "I stay here all

33

Louise with her sons Alain and Jean-Louis in 1945

The Runaway Girl

Louise has as many as three journals going at once. In them she keeps poetry, drawings, and accounts of people, events, conversations, and opinions.

———

From one of Louise Bourgeois's journals:

The Runaway Girl who never grew up.
I need no support nor comfort.
I need no safety net, no breakfast.
No lunch or tea, no visitors, no telephone calls nor little messages.
No little concerts, no hype, or encouragement for big projects.
No ambitions, no spying on my neighbors.
I need nothing . . . I can wait, I am not afraid, I am an adult.
Nothing is lacking.

year. There is safety and danger, passivity and aggression all around. This is what exhilarates me." The push and pull of opposites and the constant building and tearing down of New York stimulated her art-making. The couple lived in a small apartment in the city, and because her studio was cramped, she mostly painted and drew.

Since Robert was a respected art historian, fluent in French, a number of the Surrealist artists who had fled the rise of Nazism in Europe often gathered at their house. There they met with other New York intellectuals to discuss politics and art. Louise, who had known some of these male artists in Paris, eyed them with a certain skepticism. "I objected to them. . . . They were so lordly and pontifical."

Even in Paris when they were the most admired modern artists, she had chosen not to be one of their groupies. She said, "Since I was a runaway girl, father figures on these shores rubbed me the wrong way." While Louise rejected the Surrealists, she adapted their use of free association and fantastical organic forms. But she would go beyond their intellectual games. "The difference between me and the Surrealists," she said, "was that they saw life as a joke and I see it as a tragedy."

Moving to New York City didn't change Louise's rebellious spirit. But now she had to balance artistic ambitions with motherhood. In 1939, after a year of marriage, she and Robert had returned to Paris to adopt an orphan named Michel. Louise had convinced herself she could not get pregnant. However, a year later her son Jean-Louis was born, and the year after that, Alain. She explained that after they adopted Michel, she was able to conceive. "The anxiety was gone . . . the fear of not having children made me hysterical." When Louise worried about something, it often turned up in her art. Her painting *Natural History, 1944*, picturing three stages of a plant's evolution from growing roots to bearing fruit, refers to a woman's ability to grow, to be fertile, to reproduce.

Natural History, *1944*

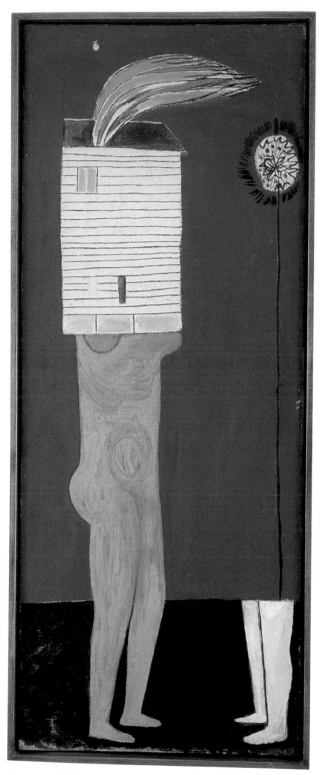

Femme Maison, *1945–47*

Natural History, 1944, was included in her first solo show in 1945 along with other prints, drawings, and paintings done in these early years. Images of the house and the female body expressed her themes of anger and abandonment, or the opposite—love and tenderness. In *Femme Maison,* the female figure carries a house covering her head. The puzzle is deciding whether the body is bursting out of the house or the house is taking over the body. She did a series of Femme Maisons, all female figures, some with hair like flames shooting out of the top. She said, "Even though I am French, I cannot think of one of these pictures being painted in France. Every one of these pictures is American, from New York. I love this city, its clean-cut look, its sky, its buildings, its scientific, cruel, romantic quality."

At a time when the highest compliment for a serious woman artist was "she paints like a man," Louise was praised by a critic for painting ". . . a world of women. Blithely they emerge from chimneys, or, terrified, they watch from beds as curtains fly from a nightmare window. A whole family of females proves their domesticity by having houses for heads."

Femme Maison could be interpreted into English as "housewife," which has many different associations for American women. "I'm *just* a housewife" was the phrase the feminists ridiculed in the 1960s, but this was the 1940s. After World War II ended in 1945, women who had labored to keep American industry running while men were off fighting were told it was patriotic to give up their jobs. They should stay at home and have children.

According to women's magazines, such as *Ladies' Home Journal* and *Good Housekeeping*, the ideal woman of the 1940s and 1950s cooked like Betty Crocker and looked like Marilyn Monroe. And here was Louise painting women who seemed imprisoned, confined, as well as sheltered by their domestic role. She wanted children and considered having them a "privilege," but art also "was a privilege given to me and I had to pursue it." Finding time to make her art meant time away from the demands of a young family. Luckily Robert turned out to be "a wonderful, reasonable man who kept the house together."

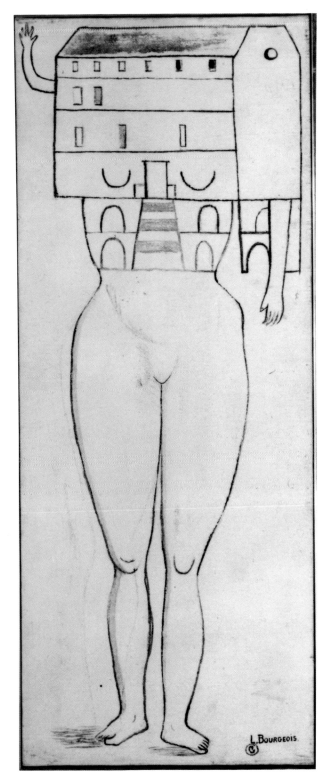

Femme Maison, *about 1946–47*

During this period, she also returned to sculpture, carving from vertical blocks of lightweight balsa wood. "You can have a family and work in wood," said Louise. "It's not dirty. It's not noisy. It's a humble, practical medium." When she grew restless, she carried her pieces from the studio up to the roof, where there was more room to work.

Simple, abstract figures, most of them between five and six feet tall, painted black, white, or red, the Personages suggest totems or African art. They formed her first one-woman show of sculpture at the Peridot Gallery in 1949. During the war, France had been occupied by the German army, and Louise, anxious about friends and family, said the Personages stand for "people I missed, all the people I left behind in France."

She took over a room in the gallery, arranging her figures singly or in small groups. Instead of placing the sculptures on a pedestal as if they existed in a separate "art space," she bolted them directly to the floor. In this way the life-sized figures seemed to take on human qualities, like people isolated yet at the same time trying to speak to one another. The viewer becomes an active participant, surrounded by art, instead of a mere observer. Although the Personages could be sold individually, together they formed an installation, to be seen as a whole. Many contemporary artists have made installation pieces since, but art historians call the Personages a first.

Not all the Personages represented friends and family in France. *Portrait of C.Y.*, 1947–49, a long wood form with two holes for eyes at the top and a cluster of nails in the chest, refers to an annoying houseguest, a woman who "drove everyone up the wall." *Portrait of Jean-Louis*, 1947–49, dedicated to one of her

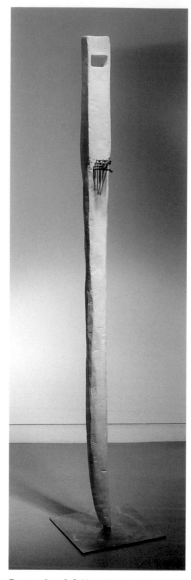

Portrait of C.Y., *1947–49*

Portrait of Jean-Louis,
1947–49

Louise on the roof of her apartment building in New York City, 1944

Louise's second show of Personages, 1950

sons, brings to mind a skyscraper with two legs, like Femme Maisons, a body merged with a building. "I wanted my son to be as beautiful as the skyscrapers in New York," she said. The next year the gallery mounted a second group of *Personages,* one of which was purchased by the Museum of Modern Art in New York—a great coup for a young artist. Ultimately, there would be a third show at the Peridot.

In *The Blind Leading the Blind,* 1947–49 two rows of tapered wood legs stand like rigid, marching soldiers who are held in formation by a platform. She said the piece symbolized "old men who drive you over the precipice. . . . Fear holds this group together. They need each other so they won't fall down." This sly reference to the Surrealists might have been prompted by the fact that although she was having some success, the New York art world still belonged to male artists.

In 1951 her father died. Louise was devastated. Despite her ambivalence toward this complex, worldly man, they shared a close bond and, after she had moved to New York, often wrote

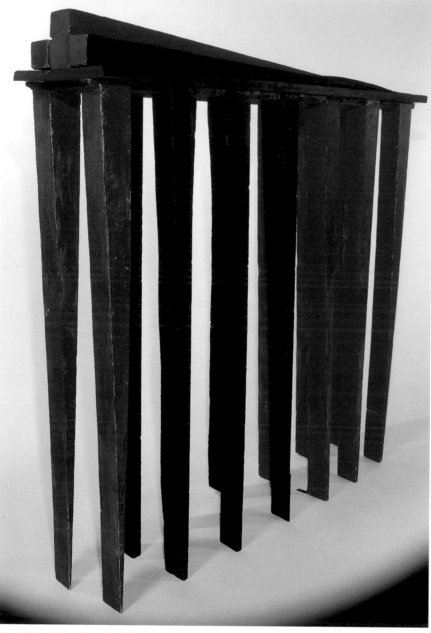

The Blind Leading the Blind, *1947–49*

Louise with her father, Louis, at Leon & Eddie's Restaurant, New York City, 1948

and visited each other. All her life she had vied for his attention, relishing her status as the favored child, the person on whom he relied. Even though she had run away from her father to New York, she could not leave behind the need to prove herself to him. With his death she withdrew from the art scene. It would be many years before she would be showcased in a New York gallery again.

Louise (wearing the hat) standing with her husband Robert Goldwater at an art show opening in the 1960s Photograph © by Fred W. McDarrah

"I would love to be articulate, because of this optimistic, way-down streak in me that believes if people knew me, they could not fail to love me— I do believe that!"

—Louise Bourgeois

CHAPTER FIVE

THE NEW YORK ART SCENE

For eleven years after the critical triumph of the two Personages exhibits, Louise's sculpture was virtually ignored. Her presence in the world of the New York movers and shakers was as the wife of a well-known art historian, not as an artist. "Because of the profession and personality of my husband, I lived among these people. And because I was French and kind of discreet they tolerated me—with my accent I was a little strange, I was not competition, and I was cute, I guess."

Occasionally she was included in a group show but remained an "artist's artist," known only to a few. Louise refused to push herself or market her sculpture. "It was just that I had the feeling that the art scene belonged to the men, and that I was in some way invading their domain. Therefore the work was hidden away."

The Lair, *1962*

Louise was not wrong. Art world attention of the 1950s focused on a kind of art called Abstract Expressionism. Painters, mostly men such as Jackson Pollock and Willem de Kooning, produced large, vigorous canvases that stressed color, line, and texture over recognizable subject matter. Pollock called his painting "energy and motion made visible." On the other hand, Louise, now in her forties, was preoccupied with sculpture, creating small objects that had narrative or storytelling qualities. She went her own solitary way, making art that was not fashionable and had little to do with what she called "macho art."

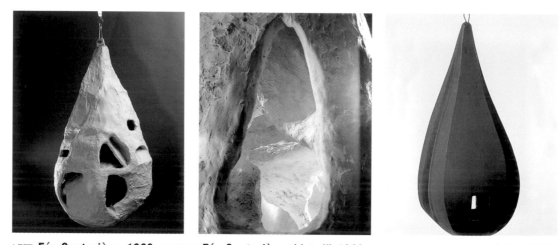

LEFT: **Fée Couturière,** *1963;* MIDDLE: **Fée Couturière,** *(detail) 1963,* Photo: Peter Moore; RIGHT: **Lair, 1986 (rubber)**

Her sculpture was moving in a startling direction. Instead of tall and angular shapes regarded as masculine and aggressive, she now turned to soft, rounded forms identified as female or nurturing. Where once she had used hard materials cut from wood, now she was pouring and modeling out of plaster, latex, and resins. Female and male private body parts melded into soft, bulbous knots that blurred gender lines. Personal and disturbing, these works are hard to look at, as if we are intruding on something we shouldn't know.

A family vacation with Robert and the boys to the Lascaux caverns in the south of France inspired some of these artworks. For Louise the caves, with a history of sheltering humans that stretched back fifteen thousand years, struck a deep chord. The series that resulted, entitled Lairs, would take its place with her Spirals, themes to be revisited again and again. Like much of Louise's work, Lairs has an element of domestic architecture. She said, "Lairs grow from within. . . . Each seems to have an internal life which causes it to grow to a certain size." The viewer can peer into the openings and see the complicated structure inside. She called them hiding places, "a safe place to put a baby," with "an entrance and an exit so you won't be trapped."

She created Lairs for many years and in many ways. "I always want to make it better. So when I have made it in plaster, I am not satisfied with that. And I say, 'If I made it in stone, would I have a better chance to communicate what I want to say?' So I will go from one material to another."

Fée Couturière, 1963, a piece made of rough plaster from her series of Lairs, hangs from the ceiling like the home of an exotic bird or a wasp's nest. "Everything goes round and round in a lair. It is a place where you are able to take care of yourself under

LEFT: **Lair, *1962–63;*** RIGHT: **Resin Eight, *1965,*** *Photo: Peter Moore*

pressure." She even fashioned Lairs out of rubber, a substance more likely to be found in a factory than in a museum.

By 1966 Louise was still working in relative obscurity when Lucy Lippard, a former student of Louise's husband, was putting together an exhibit of young, cutting-edge artists at the Fischbach Gallery in New York City. Although Lippard had heard of Louise, she was unfamiliar with her sculpture. What she saw amazed her. How, Lippard wondered, could someone so powerful, with such an original vision, have been overlooked by the art establishment? She included Louise in her groundbreaking show "Eccentric Abstraction." The other artists in the show were decades younger, but they shared Louise's preoccupation with body-focused art and offbeat materials, such as latex, rubber, and string. Louise's funky floor piece of knotted hemp, *Resin Eight*, 1965, looked right at home. It recalled the skeins of dyed wool in the Bourgeoises' tapestry workshop.

Louise's quiet reputation began to grow. The fact that Lippard had championed her work brought Louise renewed attention from critics and collectors. Although she continued to make pieces out of stuff that was unusual or discarded, she also turned to a more permanent material—marble. She made a trip to the marble quarries in Pietrasanta and Carrara, Italy. She was to go several times in the sixties, to work and pick out marble for the new sculptures that began to occupy her.

Instead of the tall, fragile figures of the Personages standing isolated in space, she carved rounded shapes clustered together. In *Cumul I* her forms burst with life as if they might grow. The surface, polished to a silky sheen, invites touching. She says, "The title *Cumul* comes from a system of clouds, and for me it's the study of clouds, of the sky of the heavens, which is something very positive, very calming . . . It is peace, the peaceful side of things."

She would go back to Pietrasanta many times in the sixties and again in the eighties. Jerry Gorovoy, who accompanied her on one such trip, says there wasn't much time for sightseeing. They arrived at their hotel in the evening and instead of going to a restaurant or walking around town, she insisted on getting right to work. Jerry says that Louise has a hard time relaxing. "If you take her to the beach, she can sit still for about five minutes. Then she gets restless." Unfortunately Louise hadn't packed any art supplies—no clay, wax, or Plasticine. So she asked Jerry for the shirt off his back. She

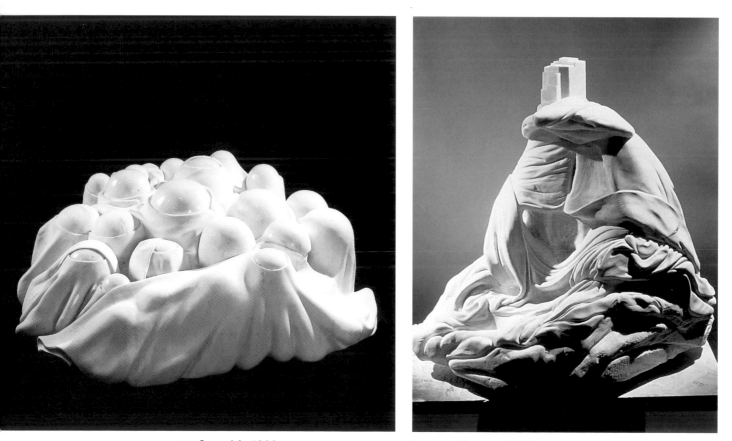

LEFT: **Cumul I,** *1969, Photo: Peter Moore;* RIGHT: **Femme Maison,** *1983*

folded and shaped it, stitching the cotton into position until she was satisfied with the form. The next day at the quarry she changed the design somewhat, then applied gesso, a liquid plaster, to harden the fabric. A larger, marble version was measured and roughed out by the craftsmen at the quarry according to her specifications. Then it was shipped to the studio, where, upon her return, she carefully re-worked it with a chisel. Eventually Jerry's shirt evolved into *Femme Maison*, 1983, a fresh interpretation of her familiar subject.

In 1973, when she was sixty-two years old and her career finally was taking off, her husband, Robert, died. Louise seldom talked about her husband or her sons, feeling they had a right to their privacy; but she said of Robert, "He was a completely rational person. He had the same qualities as my mother. He did not betray me. He did not betray anyone. I never saw him angry in my life."

With her husband gone and her

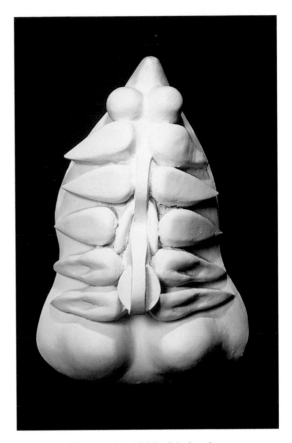

Torso, Self Portrait, *1963–64. Louise says, "This is the way I experience my torso . . . somehow with a certain dissatisfaction and regret that one's own body is not as beautiful as one would like it to be."*

children grown, Louise moved into a more public aspect of her career. A new day had dawned for women with the emergence of the Feminist movement. A surge of interest in art by and about women resulted in a reappraisal of Louise's sculpture. The rise of feminism stimulated passionate arguments about gender. Newspapers, magazine articles, and books debated the biological and cultural differences between men and women.

Discussions about gender roles were made to order for Louise. Along with taking an active part in demonstrations, panels, and exhibitions, she also put together a mock fashion show called *A Banquet/A Fashion Show of Body Parts.* Friends and students paraded in getups designed by Louise to be embarrassing only to those who took themselves too seriously. Louise herself was photographed for *Vogue* magazine wearing a tunic of latex breasts. The costume, which teased our ideas of female attractiveness, looked like the lumpy shell of a turtle or even a fertility goddess from an ancient religion.

Louise is not resentful of her many years without recognition. Quite the contrary. She said, "My first experience of great luck was that I was not picked up by the art scene and I was left to work by myself. I did not consider I was ignored. I considered that I was being blessed by privacy. My second piece of luck was my positive relation to the younger generation. My love is with them. I relate to them. There is an exchange. I give my

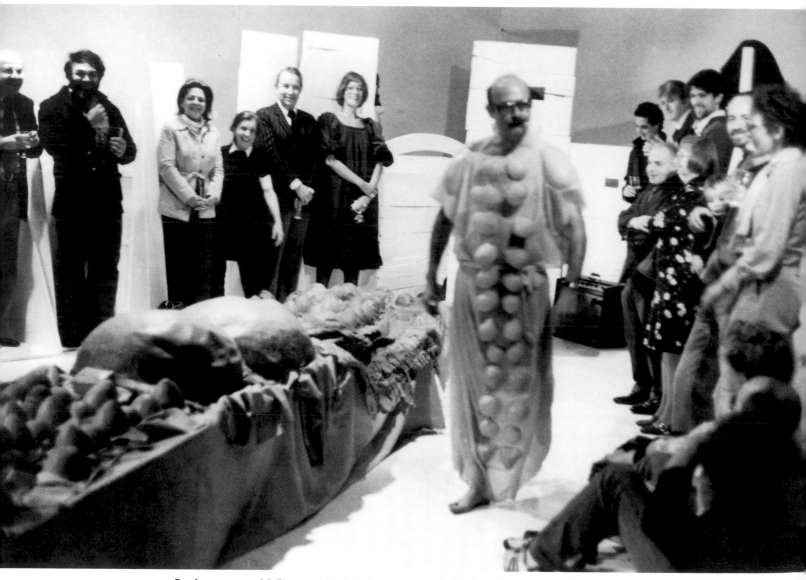

Performance of A Banquet/A Fashion Show of Body Parts *in conjunction with her piece* Confrontation, *1978, Photo: Peter Moore*

positive feelings to them." She has been a direct influence on a generation of younger artists. "You just can't deal with the human body from a psychological point of view without repeating what Louise Bourgeois has done," an artist commented in a magazine interview. Another artist, Adrian Piper, told of an incident in 1988, when she was attacked in print by a prominent critic. Feeling the review was racist and unfair, Piper answered back, publishing a rebuttal. She knew that by publicly responding to criticism she was breaking an unwritten rule. Out of the blue, Louise, whom she had never met, invited Piper to a party in her honor. Louise called for a toast, saying, "I'm sure you don't want to talk at length about the reason why we're toasting you, but we're going to toast you anyway." Piper called Louise "one of my all-time artistic heroines."

As the world grew curious about what she was up to, Louise had

The artist in a latex costume made by her, 1975

plenty to show. She always had believed in herself. For forty years what she couldn't sell was stored in her Brooklyn studio—a little dusty, but there, waiting. "Many artists destroy their work not because it is bad but because it is not successful—because other people are not interested in it." At last the world was ready for her. It was as if she had been preparing her whole adult life to be discovered overnight.

"I am kind of a secretive person. And the fantastic amount of work that I show now has been done over a period of ten or fifteen years. The idea to show does not enter the mechanism of my working."

—Louise Bourgeois

CHAPTER SIX

THE GREAT DECADE

November 1982. Crowds waited in long lines at the Museum of Modern Art (MoMA) in New York City. They were there to see the work of the first woman sculptor to be singled out for a retrospective in the museum's fifty-three-year history. More than an exhibit, a retrospective honors an artist's lifetime achievement. The

Femme Couteau, *1969–70*

headline of the review in *New York* magazine said it all: "Louise Bourgeois is finally where she belongs: among the top American sculptors, and at the apex of feminist art."

Asked if she was a feminist, Louise said she wasn't sure, but she was a woman—her art couldn't help reflecting that. Room after room was filled with art the *New York Times* called "simple yet complex . . . bubbling up from the primeval soup." Plaster Lairs

53

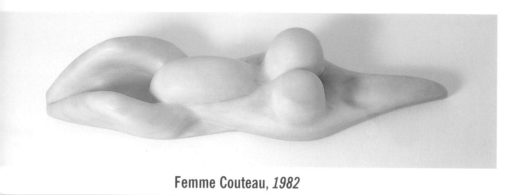

Femme Couteau, *1982*

hung from the ceiling. A niche housed *The Destruction of the Father* (see pages 18–19).

The Feminist movement embraced Louise as an example of an unjustly neglected older woman, one who had dared to produce artworks that dealt with her own body and sexuality. Her intimate, edgy sculpture was grounded in female experience, including relationships, giving birth, and motherhood. *Femme Couteau,* 1982 (a title translated as *Knife Woman*), a much-praised marble sculpture in the MoMA exhibition, lies in voluptuous folds, looking tender and defenseless. Yet, as the title tells us, she is a knife. "People say it is an aggressive form but it is not. She is armless, harmless, and very afraid. If only she knew her power," said Louise.

Fallen Woman, 1981, is armless, as well, with a beautifully carved face and a body shaped like the end of a baseball bat. "I needed a tiny chisel, especially for the eyes," said Louise, "which I found in a dental supply store. You want to protect her. She's beautiful. But because she cannot stand up, she has no purpose. . . . She never knew she was beautiful."

Women were speaking out, sharing deeply personal stories. In this welcoming environment Louise overcame her own sense of privacy. A few months before the MoMA show opened, she gave a slide show and lecture. As the photographs flashed

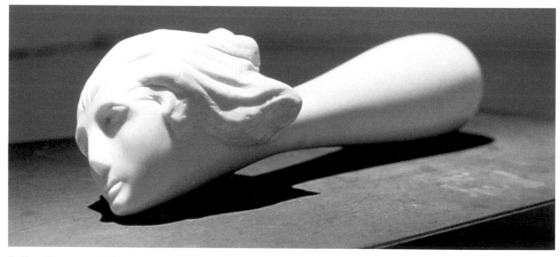

Fallen Woman, *1981*

on the screen, she shocked her audience by speaking out for the first time about her childhood; the upsetting domestic triangle of father, mother, and mistress; and the impact it had on her art making. For an artist to talk about the psychological roots of her creative process was highly unusual. Louise went from guarding her silence to orchestrating her confession. By the time the retrospective was reviewed, Louise's autobiography had become almost inseparable from people's view of her sculpture.

Even as she told her story, Louise warned her listeners to keep their eyes on the art. "An artist's words are always to be taken cautiously." Her tale, she insisted, should not be confused with the meaning of the work. "The sculpture speaks for itself and needs no explanation. My intentions are not the subject. The object is the subject. Not a word out of me is needed."

Louise was in her seventies, a time when many retire and rest on their laurels. Nothing could have been further from her mind. She said, "I am delighted with the show. It's a step and then you go beyond the step and are ready to start again."

For almost forty years she had used her hands—pouring, drilling, hacking, carving, polishing. Then one afternoon in the south of France at an outdoor flea market she and Jerry were wandering around the booths, looking at the odd assortment of merchandise for sale. Louise spotted some glass cupping jars like the ones she'd once put on

Ventouse, *1990, glass jars used for cupping arranged on a marble slab*

her mother's back. Seeing the glass cups jolted her memory, and she quickly bought all of them. Later in her New York studio, she arranged the cups on dark marble slabs, like offerings on an altar (*Ventouse,* 1990).

Articles from her past, each one holding a memory, filled her house and studio. Slowly she started recycling these "found objects" into her art—old furniture, clothing, and castoffs. Some artists scour junk stores to find things to use in their work, but Louise prefers her own treasure trove, artifacts that document her life. Needles, spindles, knives, chairs, dresses, shirts, mirrors, bottles, and more—no detail of Louise's history is forgotten. Jerry said, "She hoards things. She can't throw anything away."

She called her new series of installations Cells, and said, "When I began building the Cells, I wanted to create my own architecture and not depend on the museum space, not have to adapt my scale to it. I wanted to constitute a real space which you could enter and walk around in."

They were fabricated at her studio in Brooklyn, which had been at one time an old sewing factory. When she took it over, the factory was crammed with discarded junk, including a number of worn wooden doors. Louise saved them. Friends called and said, "They're tearing down an old building. I can get you five doors," and Louise would say, "Okay, bring them over." She used the doors for walls on some of these innovative spaces she was creating.

The first Cells dealt with the five senses. For example, a bottle of Shalimar perfume, her favorite scent, placed on a mirror in the cell, called forth the sense of smell (*Cell II*, 1991). She kept adding and changing, adding and changing. "The subject of pain is the business I am in. To give meaning and shape to frustration and suffering. The Cells represent different types of pain." Louise went on to construct cells made of open grid work, salvaged windows lined up like a wall of cages. The process evolved slowly, one thing leading to another. From the images of houses in the Femme Maison paintings to Lairs to life-sized rooms, Louise invited the viewer to peer into her architecture of memory.

Cell II, *(detail) 1991, Shalimar bottles and carved marble hands*

In *Cell (Choisy)*, 1990–93, a pink marble model of Choisy, her first childhood house, dominates the wire enclosure. Louise said it is exact, and she can show you where her bedroom once was, as well as the room of her parents. Over it looms a guillotine with blade raised. This was the machine used historically in France to cut off the heads of convicted criminals. The blade hovering over the family house speaks of the danger of memories, warns not to come too close.

Cell (Choisy), *(detail) 1990–93.* Louise says, *"Assemblage is different than carving. It is not an attack on things. It is coming to terms with things. With assemblages or the found object you are caught by a detail or something strikes your fancy and you adjust, you give in, you cut out, and you put together."*

Cell VII, *1998, includes clothes from Louise's attic and doors from the sewing machine factory.*

In *Cell VII,* 1998, the same house is cast in bronze in a cell strung with clothes from Louise's attic. These wispy garments, worn long ago, hang as ghostly reminders of times gone by. Although the artist knows who gave her the clothes and where she wore them, she is not being sentimental. She says, "To reminisce and woolgather is negative. You have to differentiate between memories. Are you going to them or are they coming to you? If you are going to them, you are wasting time. Nostalgia is not productive. If they come to you, they are the seeds for sculptures." These artworks are the visual equivalents of one of her diaries, a mixture of intense pleasure and anxiety. Picking through the piles of clothes, stringing them up, placing objects in the space, she loses herself in the pleasure of creating—resolving a problem. Unlike life, *Cell VII,* 1998, is a world she can control. And even if we don't know her story, the piece calls forth an emotional response from us.

Louise has never adhered to one style, form, or medium in her sculpture. Representing the story of her childhood in so many different ways, each new show took critics by surprise. Cut, sewn, torn, folded, welded, chiseled, cast, molded, and assembled . . . a variety of artworks created from an ability to trust her instincts and let her imagination run free.

Louise in her Brooklyn studio in 1993, with Shredder *(1983) and* Spider *(in progress)*

"My children have asked me many times, 'Where did you get that idea? That is not the way it happened.' And they tell me that I said this or that. Well, I never remotely said that. What happened in their past is up for discussion. Whereas in my childhood, nobody discusses it. It is my childhood. That is what I love."

—Louise Bourgeois

CHAPTER SEVEN

SPIDER, SPIDER, BURNING BRIGHT

Louise has trouble sleeping at night. Propped up in her bed overlooking Twentieth Street, she draws. Images of circles, snakes, flowers, flowing hair, ladders, and trees appear again and again in notebooks and diary entries. There are sketches of the meandering rivers of France, such as the Bièvre,

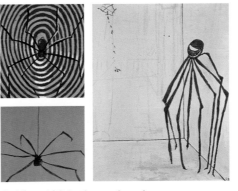

Spider, 1994, three drawings

into which she says she once threw herself when she felt particularly angry at her father. The rhythmic, repetitive pattern of these drawings weaves together her recurring themes. "What is a drawing? It is a secretion, like a thread in a spider's web. . . . It is a knitting, a spiral, a spiderweb and other significant organizations of space."

These days, in her nineties, Louise stays close to

ABOVE: **I Do** *(foreground)*, **I Redo** *(middle ground)*, **I Undo** *(background)*, *1999–2000, at the Tate Modern in London;*
OPPOSITE: **Maman,** *1999, in the Turbine Hall at the Tate Modern*

home. She says that art is about making connections, communicating, but that she is not in the entertainment business. She doesn't attend gallery openings or appear at art-world parties. "People need to see the work. It's more me than my physical presence." It is her artwork therefore that goes out into the world, circling the globe.

The Tate Modern, the largest museum for modern art in the world, opened in London in May of 2000. Louise was commissioned to do the first installation for the huge ground floor Turbine Hall. Her three gigantic steel towers—titled *I Do, I Undo,* and *I Redo*—dominated the hall. Are they architectural structures or sculptures? The answer is both, reminding us of skyscrapers, watch towers, lighthouses, or observation decks.

These pieces are grander, more monumental than earlier works. Louise made them in steel, directing a welder who came to her studio. The first models were three feet high, tacked together, almost like three-dimensional sketches. Gradually she made changes and the sculpture took shape. At that point the director of the Tate Modern came from London to see what she had planned. He liked what he saw. Then an engineer got involved to make sure her concept was structurally sound, so that people going up and down the towers would be safe.

Whether small, or large-scale, her sculpture has the power to command attention, to startle. The towers, with chairs placed on the landings, were intended to encour-

age conversation. Spectators looked up to confront their reflections in huge, over-hanging mirrors. The artist, who confronts herself every day, demanded that her view-ers do the same. Was Louise suggesting that strangers should meet in the towers and talk? She said, "It would be arrogant to say I have the power to do that, and I am not arrogant." These sculptures carry a hopeful message—that it is possible to talk, to change, and to go forward.

Almost dwarfed by the commanding towers was the sculpture everyone fell in love with—a thirty-five-foot spider, titled *Maman*, French for mother. For Louise, the spider

LEFT: **Maman,** *1999,* with **Spider,** *1996, in the plaza at Rockefeller Center, New York City, 2001;* ABOVE: **The Nest,** *1994*

is the symbol of her industrious mother, who spent her days repairing, restoring, reweaving. A guardian figure, creative, touching, and humorous. At the end of the exhibit, the London *Maman* was packed away into storage, but other *Maman*'s appeared. For one summer the giant spider of bronze, stainless steel, and marble formed an arch over a busy crossway of Rockefeller Center in New York City. Two smaller, baby spiders hovered nearby (*Spider,* 1996). They were not meant to be anatomically correct, with spiny legs like crutches. Still they had a definite spidery presence. A sac filled with eggs hung from *Maman*'s core like a chandelier. A friendly creature rather than an intimidating one, her body formed a dome-like canopy. Groups of tourists crowded together underneath to have their photographs taken. People hurrying through them with briefcases stopped for a minute to smile. Children played tag around the spindly legs. Although spiders are considered frightening creatures, Louise's spiders were a welcoming, even comical sight on this busy plaza. There was no arachnophobia there.

Topiary III, *1999*

The spider may be her mother, but it also is the artist, spinning her web, pulling the art out of herself. You can't call Louise mellow, but she has changed—loosening her hold on some of her old fear and pain. "Perhaps you wouldn't know it from my work, but I have an optimistic view of the world, that things get better."

The spiders spun an international web, appearing at the Guggenheim Museum in Bilbao, Spain; Playhouse Square in Cleveland, Ohio; and then on to the Winter Palace in St. Petersburg, Russia, where Louise was the first living American artist to have a major exhibition. There were many festivities around these openings, but Louise did not attend the celebrations. The spiders were on their own.

What happens next? That is her main focus. And so she stays at home on Twentieth Street, spinning her memories, fantasies, and ideas into art. Free with her thoughts and feelings, up to a point, she lets us know that there are other secrets, other ideas and thoughts to consider about her, about her work. "I'm a long distance runner. I'm a lonely runner and that's the way I like it."

Important Dates

1911 Louise Joséphine Bourgeois is born in Paris on Christmas Day. Her parents, Louis and Joséphine, own a tapestry restoration business. Her sister, Henriette, was born seven years earlier.

1912 The family lives in a large house outside of Paris in Choisy-le-Roi with an atelier behind it for the tapestry makers.

1913 Pierre, her brother, is born in January.

1914 World War I. France goes to war against Germany.

1915–1918 Louis Bourgeois and his brother Desiré go off to fight in the war. As a result of the war, the family moves to Aubusson. Desiré is killed during his first week of fighting. The armistice is signed in 1918. War is officially over.

1919, 1920 The Bourgeois family buys a house in Antony by the Bièvre River, which has the tannin needed to dye the tapestries. The three children attend school in Antony.

1920 Women gain the right to vote in the United States.

1921–1927 At age ten Bourgeois begins to help out in the tapestry workshop and attends the lycée in Paris.

1921 Bourgeois's education is briefly interrupted to take care of her mother, who had contracted the Spanish flu at the end of the war. They go to the south of France.

1922 Sadie Gordon, a young Englishwoman, comes to live in the Bourgeois household to be the children's tutor. She also becomes Louis Bourgeois's mistress.

1932 Her mother, Joséphine Bourgeois, dies. Bourgeois receives a degree in philosophy from the Sorbonne, part of the University of Paris.

1933–1938 Bourgeois decides to abandon her interest in mathematics to pursue art. She attends various academies and studio workshops. Marries Robert Goldwater and moves to New York City (NYC), where he is professor of art at the Institute of Fine Arts, New York University.

1939–1945 World War II.

1939 Bourgeois enrolls in the Art Students League in NYC. The Goldwaters socialize with major art-world figures, including art historians, artists, architects, and art dealers. They return to France to adopt Michel Olivier. Bourgeois exhibits in the United States for the first time in a print exhibition at the Brooklyn Museum.

1940 France is occupied by German forces. A son, Jean-Louis Bourgeois, is born.

1941 Another son, Alain Mathew Clement, is born. The family moves to Stuyvesant's Folly in NYC and buys a country house in Easton, Connecticut.

1945 First solo show of paintings at Bertha Schaefer Gallery in NYC. Exhibits at Peggy Guggenheim's gallery, NYC, in a group show and at the Whitney Museum of American Art, NYC.

1947 Completes nine engravings with parables, *He Disappeared Into Complete Silence.* Exhibits seventeen paintings, including *Femme Maison,* at Norlyst Gallery in NYC.

1949 Sculptural debut at the Peridot Gallery in NYC.

1950 Second exhibition of sculptures at the Peridot Gallery.

1950–1951 Robert Goldwater receives a Fulbright scholarship to conduct research in France. They rent a house and studio in Paris, which she has until 1955.

1951 Louis Bourgeois, Louise's father, dies. Museum of Modern Art in NYC (MoMA) acquires sculpture *Sleeping Figure.*

1953 The Goldwater family visits the caves in Lascaux, France.

1955	Louise Bourgeois becomes an American citizen.
1958	Stuyvesant's Folly is sold and torn down. The family moves to West Twenty-second Street in NYC. Louise opens Erasamus Books and Prints.
1960	Bourgeois teaches in the public schools in Great Neck, New York. She exhibits in a group show in Paris and at the Whitney Museum. Bourgeois enrolls in the Graduate School of Arts and Sciences at New York University.
1962	The Bourgeois family moves to West Twentieth Street in NYC, where she lives today.
1963	Bourgeois teaches at Brooklyn College.
1964	United States begins its major involvement in Vietnam by sending troops. After eleven years without a solo show, Bourgeois exhibits a new work at the Stable Gallery in NYC.
1966	Bourgeois is included in Lucy Lippard's show "Eccentric Abstraction."
1967-1968	Bourgeois makes her first visit to Italian marble quarries, where she regularly returns through 1972.
1970	Bourgeois involves herself in the Feminist movement, taking part in demonstrations, panels, and exhibits.
1971	National Women's Political Caucus is founded in Washington, D.C.
1973	Her husband, Robert Goldwater, dies. She exhibits in New York and Paris and designs sets and costumes for two plays.
1974	Bourgeois continues to exhibit widely and to teach at such universities as Yale, Columbia, and Rutgers.
1975	Saigon falls to North Vietnam, ending United States involvement in Vietnam.
1978	She presents her performance *A Banquet/A Fashion Show of Body Parts*.
1982	Bourgeois's retrospective opens at the MoMA in NYC. It is the first retrospective given to a woman sculptor at the museum. She makes a slide presentation entitled *Partial Recall*, telling for the first time the story of her early family history. Bourgeois exhibits with the Robert Miller Gallery through the 1980s and '90s.
1987	An exhibition of her work travels to five American museums, among them the Gallery of Art at Washington University in St. Louis.
1988	She travels to Carrara, Italy, where she begins a series of works in pink marble.
1989	Bourgeois has a number of solo exhibitions from New York City to Madrid, Spain.
1990	She is honored at the MacDowell Colony in New Hampshire. Her son Michel dies.
1991	She is awarded the Grand Prix in sculpture from France.
1992	Exhibit at the Solomon R. Guggenheim Museum in NYC. *A Homely Girl, A Life*, a collaboration between Bourgeois and Arthur Miller, is published. *She Lost It*, a fabric piece, installed at Fabric Workshop in Philadelphia.
1993	Bourgeois represents the United States at the Venice Biennale in Italy. Bourgeois is chosen by the Art Institute and City of Chicago to do a piece in honor of Jane Addams, who had founded Hull House, an educational institution for immigrants especially geared toward women and children. Honored by mayor of NYC.
1994	A print exhibition of her work takes place at the MoMA in NYC and travels to museums in Europe. Documentary produced on Bourgeois by BBC in London. Saint Louis Art Museum mounts a sculpture exhibition.
1995-1996	Three separate museum exhibitions of Bourgeois's work mounted in Sydney, Australia; Seville, Spain; and Oxford, England.
1996-2003	She receives a number of commissions, including her large-scale project for the Tate Modern in London and exhibits in galleries and museums around the world.

How to Look at a Sculpture

The simplest definition of sculpture is "a three-dimensional artwork in real space, not space that is drawn or painted." A wide range of artworks crowd into that definition. Some sculptures are self-contained; others interact with the landscape. Some can be placed anywhere—in a gallery, a museum, or a park; others are site-specific and exist in and for a chosen setting. From public sculpture to small objects, no single style or material has dominated the imagination of Louise Bourgeois. But wherever it is, no matter what material she uses—from marble to plastic, fabric to glass, wood to bronze—her sculpture engages you in an active experience.

When you look at a sculpture, ask yourself some questions.

What is the material? What are the dimensions? What is the title?
Couple is made of worn terry cloth fabric, 20 x 7 x 3 inches.

How is it made?
Couple is cut, stuffed, and hand-stitched.

What do you see? Begin by describing the artwork. Is it a figure, an object, or an abstract form?
These small figures, a male and a female, are attached to a wire hanging from the ceiling. The material is frayed, rust-colored fabric, probably recycled from Bourgeois's old bathrobe. The female hugs the male, who cannot hug back because he has no arms. She stands on tiptoes on his feet; her cheek touches his. The figures are simplified with no hair or clothes.

A sculpture is made up of color, line, form, and texture. These are the basic elements. Scale (size), proportion, distortion, and light also come into play. How is the work composed?
The proportions of *Couple* are human, but the scale is small.
The texture of *Couple* is soft and fuzzy, rubbed like a loved toy.
The lines are curvy.
The color is dull rather than bright.

What are some sensory words that describe this piece? Sensory words refer to qualities in a sculpture that are vivid in terms of sight, touch, sound, taste, or smell.
Warm, soft, rubbed, faded

What is the feeling expressed by the artist's use of color, line, form, and texture?
Couple expresses a tender and poignant feeling because of the soft material, the small scale, and the shape of the two figures huddled together as if for comfort. Although they are worn and frayed, they offer the viewer a sense of hope and human warmth. The piece is unified by the single color, material, and form.

How does knowing about Bourgeois's life add another dimension to our response to Couple?
Her use of fabric and stitching goes back to her childhood experience working with her family in the tapestry restoration business. The first doll she made as a child was of bread. Now she uses a variety of other materials.

Couple, *2001*

Where to View Artwork by Louise Bourgeois

Australia
- National Gallery of Australia, Canberra
- National Gallery of Victoria, Melbourne

Canada
- Musée d'art Contemporain de Montréal, Québec
- Ydessa Hendeles Foundation, Toronto, Ontario

England
- British Museum, London
- Tate Modern, London

United States

Colorado
- Denver Art Museum

Washington, D.C.
- Hirshhorn Museum and Sculpture Garden, Smithsonian Institution
- National Gallery of Art

Illinois
- Jane Addams Park, Chicago

Iowa
- Des Moines Art Center

Louisiana
- New Orleans Museum of Art

Maine
- Portland Museum of Art

Massachusetts
- Fogg Art Museum, Harvard University, Cambridge
- Williams College Museum of Art, Williamstown

Michigan
- The Detroit Institute of the Arts

Minnesota
- Walker Art Center and Minneapolis Sculpture Garden, Minneapolis

Missouri
- The Saint Louis Art Museum

Nebraska
- University of Nebraska, Sheldon Memorial Art Gallery and Sculpture Garden, Lincoln

New York
- Albright-Knox Art Gallery, Buffalo
- American Craft Museum, NYC
- Battery Park City Authority for the Robert F. Wagner, Jr. Park, NYC
- Brooklyn Museum
- Solomon R. Guggenheim Museum, NYC
- The Metropolitan Museum of Art, NYC
- Museum of Modern Art, NYC
- New York Public Library, NYC
- New York University, NYC
- Storm King Art Center, Mountainville
- Whitney Museum of American Art, NYC

Ohio
- The Cleveland Museum of Art

Pennsylvania
- Carnegie Museum of Art, Pittsburgh
- Philadelphia Museum of Art
- Pittsburgh Cultural Trust

Rhode Island
- Rhode Island School of Design Museum, Providence

Texas
- Modern Art Museum of Fort Worth
- Museum of Fine Arts, Houston

LEFT: **Precious Liquids,** *1992 (exterior view);* RIGHT: **Precious Liquids,** *1992 (interior view)*

Glossary

abstract   art in which the elements—line, shape, texture, or color—rather than a recognizable object have been stressed

art historian   a scholar who specializes in the history of art and artists

artifact   an object, usually with a history

atelier   a studio or workshop used by artists and craftpersons

balsa wood   a very soft, easy-to-carve, lightweight wood that often is used for models

base   the bottom part of a sculpture

bronze   a mixture of copper and tin used for casting in a mold

cast   **n.** a hollow mold from which a work of art can be made; **v.** the act of making a work of art from a hollow mold by pouring molten metal, latex, liquid plaster, or other material into the mold and letting it harden

chisel   **n.** a tool for sculpting wood or stone; **v.** the act of sculpting wood or stone

curating   the act of choosing sculptures or paintings for an exhibit or in a museum

curator   the person in charge of a museum or exhibit

de Kooning, Willem (1904–1997)   Dutch American artist, one of the leaders of the Abstract Expressionist school of painting

docent   in a museum, a person who lectures about the work

draftsman   an artist who draws precise plans for something

Duchamp, Marcel (1887–1968)   an influential French artist, a leader of both Dada and Surrealism

elements   the building blocks of art: color, line, shape, and texture (also see *visual effects*)

> **color**   red, yellow, blue, green, orange, and violet, plus black or white—and all their combinations. Primary colors are red, yellow, and blue.

> **line**   an edge or mark that traces the contours of a form

> **shape**   refers to the appearance of a particular area in a painting or sculpture, such as a circle or a square

> **texture**   refers to the surface of the artwork, especially the way it stimulates our sense of touch

exhibits and shows   an exhibition of an artist's work, usually in a museum or gallery

> **group show**   an art exhibit in which the work of many different artists is shown

> **retrospective**   an exhibit of the work of an artist over a span of time, from early to mature work

> **solo (one-woman or one-man) show**   an art exhibit in which the work of one artist is featured

form   often used interchangeably with shape but refers specifically to the three-dimensional quality or volume of a shape

found objects   an existing object found or selected by the artist and incorporated into a work of art

gallery   a place for showing and viewing artworks

hemp   fibers from the hemp plant, often made into rope

installation   art that is built or installed in a specific room or area—can be temporary or permanent

latex   a rubberlike liquid that can be poured and then hardened

Léger, Fernand (1881–1955)   French Cubist artist

materials   the many things an artist uses to make art, from paint and stone and metal to found objects

medium   the material an artist chooses to work in, whether paint, wood, bronze, marble, or fabric

model   **n.** a small preliminary version of a sculpture; **v.** the act of making or modeling materials into sculpture

modeling   building up or manipulating material such as clay or wax; the act of sitting for a painting or sculpture; **life modeling:** an artist working from a living model

mount/mounted   to present a show of art or sculpture

organic having the physical structure characteristic of living organisms or that which even though inanimate reminds us of a living form

pedestal structure what a sculpture stands on that sets it apart from its surroundings

plaster a preparation of the mineral gypsum that is ground into a fine powder and mixed with liquid (usually water) to make a mold

Plasticine a flexible, claylike material that can be easily modeled

Pollock, Jackson (1912–1956) American Abstract Expressionist painter best known for his "drip" paintings

principles of art another way of referring to visual effects, or balance, emphasis, rhythm, space, unity, and variety

print an art that is made in multiples such as an etching

proportion the relationship of the parts of a sculpture to one another and to the sculpture as a whole

quarry a place where stone is cut and mined

realistic art sculpture (or painting) with a recognizable subject that imitates life

repetition see *visual effects*

resin a liquid material that dries clear, derived either from plants or from natural synthetics

rhythm see *visual effects*

scale 1. how the size of a sculpture compares to human scale; 2. how it relates to the room, the building, or the site

sepia a brown-toned photograph or drawing

series a group of works by an artist that explore a theme or materials in a variety of ways

shape the appearance of a particular area in a sculpture or painting

skein a bundle of yarn or thread, usually wrapped in long loops

sketch a rough, often preliminary drawing done as a study or outline of an object or scene

space one of the ways to talk about a work of sculpture

> *negative space* the empty area in a sculpture

> *positive space* the enclosed area surrounded or defined by the negative space

studio a space where an artist works

style characteristic manner or appearance of works of individual artists, groups of artists who work in a related way (schools) or periods of art

three-dimensional having, or appearing to have, length, width, and depth

visual effects the principles of design by which the elements in a sculpture or painting are arranged. Compositional devices, among them balance, emphasis, rhythm, space, unity, and variety,

> *emphasis* the element that is stressed or most prominent in a work of art

> *formal balance* the symmetrical arrangement of the elements of a work of art

> *informal balance* the asymmetrical arrangement of the elements of a work of art. The human eye seems to have an inborn ability to tell when something is balanced or in equilibrium; artists often play with this sense.

> *rhythm* movement suggested by repeating elements: visual pattern—for example, the repetition of a shape or a color in a work of art to create an effect, or the alternating of a shape with another shape or shapes to the same end

> *space* see *space*

> *unity* the harmonious or visually satisfying blending of all the visual effects in a work of art

> *variety* the many elements or the diversity of one element within a work of art; for example, the use of a number of different shapes or colors to provide contrast and visual interest

Bibliography

Articles

Sischy, Ingrid. "Louise Bourgeois." *Interview* (October 1997).

Vendrame, Simona. "Louise Bourgeois." *Tema Celeste* (May–June 2001).

Brensen, Michael. "A Sculptor Comes Into Her Own." *The New York Times* (October 31, 1982).

Books

Bernadac, Marie-Laure, and Hans-Ulrich Obrist, eds. *Louise Bourgeois, Destruction of the Father, Reconstruction of the Father, Writings and Interviews 1923–1997*, Cambridge: The MIT Press, 1998.

Bourgeois, Louise, with a story by Raymond Carver. Catalog from Cheim & Read, New York. 2001.

Bourgeois, Louise, and Lawrence Rinder. *Louise Bourgeois: Drawings & Observations*. Boston: Bulfinch Press, 1995.

Gardner, Paul. *Louise Bourgeois*. New York: Universe Publishing, 1994.

Gorovoy, Jerry, and Pandora Tabatabai Asbaghi, eds. Critical text by Paulo Herkenhoff. *Louise Bourgeois: Blue Days and Pink Days*. Milan: Fondazione Prada, 1997.

Hughes, Robert. *American Visions: The Epic History of Art in America*. New York: Alfred A Knopf, 1997.

Kotik, Charlotta, Terrie Sultan, and Leigh Christian. *Louise Bourgeois: The Locus of Memory: Works 1983–1994*. New York: Harry N. Abrams and The Brooklyn Museum, 1994.

Kuspit, Donald. *Bourgeois*. New York: Vintage, 1988.

Louise Bourgeois. London: Tate Gallery Publishing, 2000.

Louise Bourgeois: Memory and Architecture. Catalog from Museo Nacional Centro de Arte Reina Sofia, Madrid. November 16, 1999–February 14, 2000.

Louise Bourgeois Recent Works. Catalog from Malmo Konsthall and Cape Musée d'art Contemporain, Bordeaux; Centro Cultural, Belém; and Serpentine Gallery, London, 1997.

Munro, Eleanor. *Originals: American Women Artists*. New York: Simon & Schuster, 1979.

Endnotes

KB=*Bourgeois* by Donald Kuspit.

LBG=*Louise Bourgeois* by Paul Gardner.

TC="Louise Bourgeois" by Simona Vendrame (*Tema Celeste*).

LBT=*Louise Bourgeois* (Tate Gallery Publishing).

BDPD=*Louise Bourgeois: Blue Days and Pink Days* Jerry Gorovoy, Pandora Tabatabai Asbaghi, eds. Critical text by Paulo Herkenhoff.

LBDF=*Louise Bourgeois, Destruction of the Father, Reconstruction of the Father, Writings and Interviews 1923–1997*. Marie-Laure Bernadac and Hans-Ulrich Obrist, eds.

D & O=*Louise Bourgeois: Drawings & Observations*.

LBMA= *Louise Bourgeois: Memory and Architecture*. Catalog from Museo Nacional Centro de Arte Reina Sofia, Madrid.

LM=*Louise Bourgeois: The Locus of Memory* by Charlotta Kotik,Terrie Sultan, and Christian Leigh.

IS="Louise Bourgeois" by Ingrid Sischy (*Interview* magazine).

NYT=*The New York Times* (Oct. 31,1982)

O="*Originals: American Women Artists*" by Eleanor Munro.

All other quotes are from the authors' interviews with Louise Bourgeois and Jerry Gorovoy.

Chapter 1

p. 7 "I was in effect a runaway girl … " LBMA p. 15

p. 7 "In my art, I am the murderer … " LBDF p. 227

p. 7 "As an artist I am a powerful person … " LBDF p. 227

p. 7 "All my work in the past fifty years … " BDPD p. 14

p. 8 "I was a pain in the ass when I was born … " BDPD p. 14

p. 8 "When I was born, my father and mother … " LBMA p. 40

p. 10 *The Garden* O p. 158

p. 10 "I've always had a fascination …" BDPD p. 218

p. 13 "It was quite impressive …" LM p. 23

p. 13 "My parents worked together …." BDPD p. 30

p. 13 "At school art was important…" IS

p. 13 "It taught me …" KB p. 5

Chapter 2

p. 15 "You see. I have to feel …" BDPD p. 17

p. 16 "But wait," he said …" D & O p. 165.

p. 16 "I took white bread …" LBMA p. 31

p. 17 "Art is the promise …" LBMA p. 31

p. 18 "This piece is basically a table …" BDPD p. 142

p. 20 "Louise, you do not have to fear …" LBDF p. 119

p. 22 "My best friend was my mother …" DFRF p. 321

p. 22 "When my mother said something …" LBDF p. 113

p. 22 "To please my father …" IS

p. 24 "How is it that a middle-class …" LBMA p. 31

p. 25 "As you move up close …" LBDF p. 155

Chapter 3

p. 27 "I was looking for truth, for people who weren't phony, looking for authenticity." BDPD p. 64

p. 27 "My parents treated me …" LBDF p. 95

p. 28 "Mathematics…It simply went into a theoretical world …" LBG p. 22

p. 30 "I still choke with loneliness…" BDPD p. 64

p. 30 "It happened this way: one day he took a wood shaving …." BDPD p. 66

p. 31 "I was attracted to Communism …" BDPD p. 70

p. 31 "In between conversations about Surrealism …" LBDF p. 30

p. 31 "I had met someone who was kind …" O p. 62

Chapter 4

p. 33 "Do you know the New York sky?..."(The Puritan, 1947) LBDF p. 51

p. 33 "I stay here all year …." LBG p. 25

p. 34 "I objected to them ….They were so lordly and pontifical …." BDPD p. 106

p. 34 *The Runaway Girl* LBDF p. 365

p. 35 "Since I was a runaway girl, father …" BDPD p. 106

p. 35 "The difference between me and the Surrealists …" IS

p. 35 "The anxiety was gone …" LBG p. 44

p. 36 "Even though I am French..." BDPD p. 84

p. 36 "She paints like a man," Louise was praised by a critic for painting ". . . a world of women. Blithely they emerge from chimneys …" KB p. 70

p. 38 "You can have a family and work in wood," said Louise. "It's not dirty. It's not noisy. It's a humble, practical medium." NYT

p. 42 "old men who drive you over the precipice …." BDPD p. 105

Chapter 5

p. 45 "I would love to be articulate … DF p. 111

p. 45 "Because of the profession and personality of my husband …" LBDF p. 165

p. 45 "It was just that I had the feeling that the art scene ..." O p. 156

p. 49 "He was a completely rational person …" BDPD p. 73

p. 50 "My first experience of great luck …" BDPD p. 260

p. 51 "I'm sure you don't want to talk at length …" LM p. 79

p. 51 "Many artists destroy their work not because it is bad but because it is not successful—because other people are not interested in it." KB p. 73

Chapter 6

p. 54 "People say it is an aggressive form but it is not.

p. 54 "I needed a tiny chisel …" LBG p. 82

p. 55 "I am delighted with the show. It's a step and then you go beyond the step and are ready to start again." NYT

p. 55 "I don't really see why the artist should say anything …" LBDF p. 15

p. 56 "The subject of pain …" BDPD p. 196

p. 57 "Assemblage is different …" DFRF p.142

p. 59 "To reminisce and woolgather … BDPD p271

Chapter 7

p. 61 "What is a drawing? …" LBT p. 50

p. 65 "Perhaps you wouldn't know it …" TC p. 53

p. 65 "I'm a long distance runner …" LBDF p. 261

List of Artworks in Chronological Order

Louise usually works in series, often returning over many years to a familiar theme, such as Femme Maison, with new materials and ideas. In telling her story we did not present the artwork chronologically; we offer this list (with page numbers) for those who wish to consider the work in sequence.

Natural History, 1944, Oil on canvas, page 35
Untitled, 1944, Gouache on paper, page 12
Femme Maison, 1945–47, Oil and ink, page 36
Femme Maison, 1946–47, Ink on linen, page 37
Portrait of Jean-Louis, 1947–49, Bronze, page 38
Portrait of C.Y., 1947–49, Bronze and nails, page 38
The Blind Leading the Blind, 1947–49, Painted wood, page 42
Segmented Wooden Personages, 1951, page 29
The Lair, 1962, Bronze, page 45
Lair, 1962–63, Plaster, page 47
Fée Couturière, 1963, Bronze with white paint, page 46
Torso, Self Portrait, 1963–64, Bronze, page 49
Resin Eight, 1965, Resin over hemp, page 47
Cumul I, 1969, White marble, page 48
Femme Couteau, 1969–70, Carved pink marble, page 53
The Destruction of the Father, 1974, Plaster, latex, wood, and fabric, pages 18–19
Latex costume, 1975, page 51
A Banquet/A Fashion Show of Body Parts, 1978, page 50
Fallen Woman, 1981, Carrara marble, page 54
Femme Couteau, 1982, Pink marble, page 54
Femme Maison, 1983, page 48
The She-Fox, 1985, Black marble, page 24
Lair, 1986, Rubber, page 46
J'y Suis, J'y Reste, 1990, Pink marble, glass, and metal, page 30
Orange Episode, 1990, Oil, gouache, and orange collage, page 15
Ventouse, 1990, Marble, glass, and electrical light, page 55
Cell (Choisy), (detail), 1990–93, Marble, metal and glass, page 57
Cell I, (detail), 1991, Mixed media, page 27
Cell II, (detail), 1991, page 56
Le Défi, 1991, Glass, wood, electric light, page 23
Precious Liquids, 1992, Wood, metal, glass, alabaster, cloth, water, page 69
Red room (Child), 1994, page 11
Spider, 1994, (Three drawings), page 61
The Nest, 1994, Steel, page 64
Spider IV, 1996, Steel wall relief, page 22
Passage Dangereux, 1997, Mixed media, pages 12–13
Cell VII, 1998, Mixed media, page 58
Champfleurette #2, 1999, Etching, watercolor, gouache, crayon & pencil on paper, page 3
Topiary III, 1999, page 65
Maman, 1999, Bronze, page 64
Maman, 1999, Steel, page 63
I Do, I Undo, and *I Redo,* 1999–2000, page 62
Couple, 2001, Fabric, page 68

List of Artworks by Chapter

All photographs are courtesy of the artist and Cheim & Read, New York.

Front Matter

Page 3. *Champfleurette # 2*, 1999. Etching, watercolor, gouache, crayon & pencil on paper, 14⅛ x 16⅛", 35.9 x 41 cm. Collection of Wendy Williams, New York. Photograph by Christopher Burke.

Chapter 1

Page 11. *Red Room (Child)*, 1994. Mixed media, 83 x 139 x 108", 210.8 x 353 x 274.3 cm. Collection Musee d'Art Contemporain de Montreal. Photo by Marcus Schneider.

Page 12–13. (upper) *Passage Dangereux*, 1997. Mixed media, 104 x 140 x 345", 264.1 x 355. 6 x 876.3 cm. Collection of Hauser & Wirth, St. Gallen, Switzerland. Photograph by Anders Allsten. (lower) *Untitled*, 1944, Gouache on paper, 13 x 10", 33 x 23.3 cm. Private Collection. Photograph by Zindman Fremont.

Chapter 2.

Page 15. *Orange Episode*, 1990. Oil, gouache, and orange collage on board, 17 x 13⅛", 43.1 x 13 125 cm. Collection of Jerry Gorovoy, New York. Photograph by Beth Phillips.

Page 19 (upper) *The Destruction of the Father (detail)*, 1974. Plaster, latex, wood and fabric, 93⅝ x 142⅝ x 97⅞", 237.8 x 362.3 x 248.6 cm. Photograph by Peter Moore. (lower) *The Destruction of the Father*, 1974. Plaster, latex, wood, and fabric, 93⅝ x 142⅝ x 97⅞", 237.8 x 362.3 x 248.6 cm. Photograph by Rafael S. Lobato.

Page 20. *Spiral Woman (detail)*, 1984. Bronze, 19 x 4 x 5½", 48.3 x 10.2 x 14 cm; slate disc: 1¼" high x 34" diameter; 3.17 x 86.3 cm diameter. Photograph by Christopher Burke.

Page 22. *Spider IV*, 1996. Steel wall relief, 80 x 71 x 21". Collection of Jerry Gorovoy, New York. Photograph by Peter Bellamy.

Page 23. *Le Défi*, 1991. Painted wood, glass, electric light, 67½ x 58 x 26", 171.4 x 147.3 x 66 cm. Collection of Guggenheim Museum, New York. Photograph by Peter Bellamy.

Page 24. *The She-Fox*, 1985. Black marble, 70½ x 27 x 32", 179.1 x 68.6 x 81.3 cm. Photograph by Peter Bellamy.

Chapter 3

Page 27. *Cell I,(detail)*, 1991. Mixed media, 83 x 96 x 108", 210.8 x 243.8 x 274.3 cm. Daros Collection. Photograph by Peter Bellamy.

Page 29. *Segmented Wood Personages*, 1951. Estate of Peter Moore.

Page 30. *J'y Suis, J'y Reste*, 1990. Pink marble, glass, and metal, 35 x 40½ x 31", 88.9 x 102.8 x 78.7 cm. Photograph by Jochen Littkemann.

Chapter 4

Page 35. *Natural History*, 1944. Oil on canvas, 26 x 44", 66 x 111.8 cm. Photograph by Christopher Burke.

Page 36. *Femme Maison*, 1945–47. Oil and ink on canvas, 36 x 14", 91.4 x 35.6 cm. Collection of Agnes Gund, New York. Photograph by Rafael Lobato.

Page 37. *Femme Maison*, 1946–47. Ink on linen; 36 x 14", 91.44 x 35.56 cm. Collection of Ella M. Foshay, New York. Photograph by Donald Greenhaus.

Page 38. (left) *Portrait of Jean-Louis*, 1947–49. Bronze, 35 x 5 x 4", 88.9 x 12.7 x 10.2 cm. Photograph by Christopher Burke. (right) *Portrait of C.Y.*, 1947–49. Bronze and nails, 66¼ x 12 x 12", 168.3 x 12 x 12 cm. Photograph by Christopher Burke.

Page 42. *The Blind Leading the Blind*, 1947–49. Painted Wood. 67⅛ x 64⅜ x 16¼", 170.5 x 163.5 x 41.3 cm Collection of Ginny Williams Family Foundation. Photograph by Christopher Burke, courtesy of the artist.

Chapter 5

Page 45. *The Lair*, 1962. Bronze 14 x 13 x 14", 35.6 x 33 x 35.6 cm. Photograph by Peter Bellamy.

Page 46. (left) *Fée Couturière #19630*. Bronze, painted white 39½ x 22½", 100.3 x 57.2 cm. Photograph by Peter Bellamy. (middle) *Fée Couturière*, (detail) 1963. Bronze, painted white, 39½ x 22½ x 22½", 100 x 57.2 x 57.2 cm. Photograph by Peter Moore. (right) *Lair* 1986, Rubber. 43 x 21 x 21", 109.2 x 53.3 x 53.3 cm. Photograph by James Dil.

Page 47. (left) *The Lair*, 1962–63. Plaster, 18½ x 29⅛ x 21⅜", 46.9 x 73.9 x 54.2 cm. Photograph by Christopher Burke. (right) *Resin Eight*, 1965. Resin over hemp. Photograph by Peter Moore.

Page 48 (left) *Cumul I,* 1969. White marble, 22⅜ x 50 x 48". Collection Musée national d'art moderne, Centre Georges Pompidou, Paris. Photograph by Peter Moore. (right) *Femme Maison,* 1983. Marble, 25 x 19½ x 23", 63.5 x 49.5 x 58.4 cm. Collection of Jean-Louis Bourgeois, New York. Photograph by Allan Finkelman.

Page 49. *Torso, Self Portrait,* 1963–64. Bronze 24¾ x 16 x 7⅞", 62.8 x 40.6 x 20 cm. Photograph by Allan Finkelman.

Page 50. *A Banquet/A Fashion Show of Body Parts,* in conjunction with the piece *Confrontation,* 9/16 to 10/21/78. Photograph by Peter Moore.

Chapter 6

Page 53. *Femme Couteau,* 1969–1970. Carved pink marble, 3½ x 26⅜ x 4⅞", 8.9 x 67 x 12.4 cm. Emily and Jerry Spiegel Collection. Photograph by Allan Finkelman.

Page 54. (upper) *Femme Couteau,* 1982. Pink marble, 2¾ x 15¼ x 4", 7 x 38.7 x 10.2 cm. Collection of Ellen Kern, New York City. Photograph by Rafael S. Lobato. (lower) *Fallen Woman,* 1981. Carved Carrara marble, 3¾ x 4 x 13", 9.525 x 10.16 x 34.29 cm. Private Collection, Connecticut. Photograph by Allan Finkelman.

Page 55. *Ventouse,* 1990. Marble, glass, and electric light, 34 x 32 x 78", 86.3 x 81.2 x 198.1 cm. Photograph by Peter Bellamy.

Page 56. *Cell II,* 1991. Mixed media, 83 x 60 x 60", 210.8 x 150.4 x 152.4 cm. Carnegie Museum of Art, Pittsburgh. Photograph by Peter Bellamy.

Page 57. *Cell (Choisy),* 1990–93. Marble, metal, and glass, 120½ x 67 x 95", 306.1 x 170.2 x 241.3 cm. Collection of Ydessa Hendeles Art Foundation, Toronto Canada. Photograph by Peter Bellamy.

Page 58–59. *Cell VII,* 1998. Mixed media 81½ x 87 x 83", 207 x 220.9 x 210.8 cm. Flick Collection, Zurich.

Chapter 7

Page 61. (Upper left) *Spider,* 1994. Watercolor and gouache on paper. 11¾ x 11¾", 29.8 x 29.2 cm. Private collection. Photograph by Beth Phillips. (lower left) *Spider,* 1994. Watercolor & ink on paper, 11½ x 11¾", 29.2 x 29.8 cm. Collection of Werner Welle, Germany. Photograph by Beth Phillips. (right) *Spider,* 1994. Watercolor, pencil, and gouache on paper, 10 x 8", 25.3 x 20.3 cm. Collection of John Eric Cheim, New York City. Photograph by Beth Phillips.

Page 62. *I Do,* 1999–2000. Steel, stainless steel, fabric, glass, and wood, 650 x 236 x 236", 1651 x 600 x 600 cm. Photograph by Marcus Leith. *I Redo,* 1999–2000. Steel, stainless steel, marble, fabric, glass and wood, 689 x 354 x 236", 1750 x 899.7 x 600 cm. Photograph by Marcus Leith. *I Undo,* 1999–2000. Steel, stainless steel, wood, glass, and epoxy. 512 x 177 x 138", 1300.4 x 450.2 x 350.5 cm. Photograph by Marcus Leith.

Page 63. *Maman,* 1999. Steel and marble, 365 x 351 x 403", 927.1 x 891.5 x 1023.6 cm. This was shown in Tate Modern, London "Louise Bourgeois Inaugural Installation of the Tate Modern at Turbine Hall" (5/12/00–11/26/00). Photograph by Marcus Leith.

Page 64. (left) Rockefeller Center, New York City "Louise Bourgeois: Spiders" (6/21/01–9/4/01). Front: *Spider* (1996, 11" high). Center: *Maman* (1999, 30' 5" high). Back: *Spider* (1996, 10' 7" high). Organized in association with the Public Art Fund, courtesy Cheim & Read, New York. Photo: Christopher Burke. (right) *The Nest,* 1994. Steel, 101 x 1809 x 158". Collection the San Francisco Museum of Modern Art. Photograph courtesy of Musée d'Art Moderne de la Ville de Paris, France.

Page 65. *Topiary III,* 1999. Steel, fabric, beads, and wood, 27 x 20 x 21", 68.6 x 50.8 x 53.3 cm. Private Collection, Texas. Photograph by Christopher Burke.

Backmatter

Page 68. *Couple,* 2001. Fabric, hanging piece, 20 x 6½ x 3", 50 x 16.5 x 7.6 cm. Photograph by Christopher Burke.

Page 69. (exterior view) *Precious Liquids,* 1992. Wood, metal, glass, alabaster, cloth, water, 167½ x 175¼", 425.4 x 445.1 cm. Collection of Musée national d'art moderne Centre Pompidou. Photograph by Rafael Lobato. (interior view) *Precious Liquids,* 1992 Wood, metal, glass, alabaster, cloth, water, 167½ X 175¼", 425.4 x 445.1 cm. Collection of Musée national d'art moderne, Centre Georges Pompidou, Paris. Photograph by Frédéric Delpech.

Photography Credits

title page: Photo: Yosef Adar; *page 4:* Photo: Studio Fotografico, Carrara; *page 6:* Courtesy of the Louise Bourgeois Studio; *page 7:* Photo: Jean-François Jaussaud; *page 8:* Courtesy of the Louise Bourgeois Studio; *page 9 (upper):* Photo: Peter Bellamy; *page 9 (lower):* Courtesy of the Louise Bourgeois Studio; *page 10:* Courtesy of the Louise Bourgeois Studio; *page 14:* Courtesy of the Louise Bourgeois Studio; *page 16:* Photo: Claudio Edinger; *page 18:* Courtesy of the Louise Bourgeois Studio; *page 20 (lower):* Courtesy of the Louise Bourgeois Studio; *page 21:* Courtesy of the Louise Bourgeois Studio; *page 26:* Courtesy of the Louise Bourgeois Studio; *page 28:* Photo: Brassaï; *page 31:* Courtesy of the Louise Bourgeois Studio; *page 32:* Courtesy of the Louise Bourgeois Studio; *page 33:* Courtesy of the Louise Bourgeois Studio; *page 34:* Courtesy of the Louise Bourgeois Studio; *page 39:* Courtesy of the Louise Bourgeois Studio; *page 40–41:* Photo: Aaron Siskind; *page 43:* Courtesy of the Louise Bourgeois Studio; *page 44:* Copyright © by Fred W. McDarrah; *page 51:* Photo: Estate of Peter Moore; *page 52:* Photo: Jean-François Jaussaud; *page 60:* Photo: Nancy Crampton; *page 77:* Photo: Christopher Burke; *page 79:* Photo: Yosef Adar

Show of new work, November 2001 at Cheim & Read, New York City

Acknowledgments

We first met Louise Bourgeois more than ten years ago to interview her for our book in progress *The Sculptor's Eye.* In her house in Chelsea, surrounded by the many objects accumulated during her long life, she told us extraordinary stories about herself and her art. She made us laugh. She took our breath away. When we emerged, exhilarated, from her quiet living room onto the hot summer street, we knew that someday we wanted to devote a whole book to this remarkable artist and her work.

Louise is a strong woman. Without that strength, she would not have persevered during the many years before her art became widely celebrated. She also is a vulnerable woman. Her art documents her struggles with painful childhood memories and a complicated twentieth-century life. Violent, intimate, confrontational, and witty, the art she has made during her more than fifty productive years has made her an influential role model for many young women—and men—artists starting out today. We are grateful for the opportunity to have been invited back to meet with her again for *Runaway Girl.*

Special thanks to Jerry Gorovoy for his continuing interest in this project and invaluable insights into Louise's life and work. Thanks to Wendy Williams and her thoughtful and efficient efforts in providing photos and transparencies . . . to our unflappable editor Howard Reeves, his enthusiastic assistant Linas Alsenas, to our affable art director Becky Terhune, and our creative designer Anna Christian. Thanks also to Cheim & Read Gallery in New York. We are grateful to our perceptive first readers, Ani Chamichian, Nan Jordan, and Jeanne Greenberg Rohatyn.

Louise in her Brooklyn studio with her assistant, Jerry Gorovoy, in 1990

Index

Page numbers in bold indicate illustrations.

Abstract Expressionism, 46
Académie de la Grande-Chaumière, 28
African art, 38
Antony, **9**, 9–10
Aubusson, 9

A Banquet/A Fashion Show of Body Parts,
    1978, 49, **50**
Bièvre River, 9, **10**, **20**, 61
Blind Leading the Blind, The, 1947–49,
    42, **42**
Bourgeois, Joséphine, **8**, **14**, **21**
Bourgeois, Louis, 9, **14**, 31, 42–43, **43**
Bourgeois, Louise, **4**, **7**, **16**, **20**, **22**, **24**, **26**,
    28, **31**, **32**, **33**, **34**, **39**, **43**, **44**, **51**, **52**,
    60, **79**
Bourgeois, Pierre, **20**
Brassai, 28

Cell (Choisy), 1990–93, 56, **57**
Cell II, 1991, **56**
Cells, 56
Cell VII, 1998, **58**, 59
Champleurette #2, 1999, **3**
Cheim & Read, **77**
Choisy, 56
Choisy-le-Roi, **8**, 8–9
color, 22
Communism, 31
Confrontation, 1978, **50**
Couple, 2001, **68**
Crocker, Betty, 37
Cumul I, 1969, 48, **48**

Dadaism, 28
de Kooning, Willem, 46
Destruction of the Father, The, 1974, 17,
    18, **18**, **19**, 54
Drawings & Observations, 12
Duchamp, Marcel, 28
dyes, 22

École des Beaux-Arts, 28, 31

Fallen Woman, 1981, 54, **54**
Fée Couturière, 1963, **46**, 47
feminist movement, 54
Femme Couteau, 1969–70, **53**
Femme Couteau, 1982, 54, **54**
Femme Maison, 36–37
Femme Maison, 1945–47, **36**

Femme Maison, 1983, **48**, 49
Femme Maison, about 1946–47, **37**
Fischbach Gallery, 47
found objects, 55
French Riviera, 14

garden, 10
Goldwater, Alain, **34**
Goldwater, Jean-Louis, **34**, 35
Goldwater, Michel, 35
Goldwater, Robert, 31, **31**, **44**
Good Housekeeping, 37
Gordon, Sadie, **20**, 20–25
Gorovoy, Jerry, 7, 48, **79**
Guggenheim Museum, 65
guillotine, 56

I Do, 1999–2000, 62, **62**
I Redo, 1999–2000, 62, **62**
I Undo, 1999–2000, 62, **62**

J'y Suis, J'y Reste, 1990, **30**

Ladies' Home Journal, 37
Lair, 1962–63, **47**
Lair, 1986, **46**
Lair, The, 1962, **45**
Lairs, 46–47
Lascaux, 46
Le Défi, 1991, **23**
Léger, Fernand, 30
Lippard, Lucy, 47
Louvre museum, 30

Maman, 1999, **63**, **64**, 64–65
marble, 47–48
Monroe, Marilyn, 37
Museum of Modern Art (MoMA), 42,
    53–54
mythology, 10

Natural History, 1944, **35**, 35–36
Nazism, 34
Nest, The, 1994, **64**
New York City, 33–35
New York magazine, 53
New York Times, 53

Orange Episode, 1990, **15**

Passage Dangereux, 1997, **12–13**
Peridot Gallery, 38
Personages, **40–41**, 42, 45, 48

Picasso, Pablo, 31
Pietrasanta, 47–48
Piper, Adrian, 51
Playhouse Square, 65
Pollack, Jackson, 46
Portrait of C.Y., 1947–49, 38, **38**
Portrait of Jean-Louis, 1947–49, 38, **38**
Precious Liquids, 1992, **69**

R. Mutt, 28
Red Room (Child), 1994, **11**
Resin Eight, 1965, 47, **47**
Riviera, 24
Rockefeller Center, 65
runaway girl, 34

Segmented Wood Personages, 1951, **29**
Seine River, 33
Shalimar, 56
She-Fox, The, 1985, **24**, 25
Shredder, 1983, **60**
Sorbonne, 27
Spanish flu, 24
Spider, **60**
Spider, 1994, **61**
Spider, 1996, **64**, 65
Spider IV, 1996, **22**
Spirals, 46
Spiral Woman, 1984, **20**
Surrealism, 28, 34–35

tapestries, 9–10, 13, 22
Tate Modern, 62
Topiary III, 1999, **65**
Torso, Self Portrait, 1963–64, **49**
totems, 38

University of Paris, 27
Untitled, 1944, **12**

Ventouse, 1990, 55, **55**
Vogue, 49–50

Winter Palace, 65
World War I, 8
World War II, 37